The
SHAMAN'S
SPIRIT

The SHAMAN'S SPIRIT

DISCOVERING THE WISDOM OF NATURE, POWER ANIMALS, SACRED PLACES AND RITUALS

MIKE WILLIAMS

WATKINS PUBLISHING
LONDON

For Debbie Wander

The Shaman's Spirit
Mike Williams

First published in the UK and USA in 2013 by
Watkins Publishing Limited
Sixth Floor
75 Wells Street
London W1T 3QH

A member of Osprey Group

Managing Editor: Sandra Rigby
Senior Editor: Fiona Robertson
Managing Designer: Suzanne Tuhrim
Picture Research: Susannah Stone
Production: Uzma Taj

A CIP record for this book is available from the
British Library

ISBN: 978-1-78028-494-1

10 9 8 7 6 5 4 3 2 1

Typeset in EideticSerif and Instanter
Colour reproduction by XY Digital
Printed in Singapore by Imago

Notes:
Abbreviations used throughout this book:
CE Common Era (the equivalent of AD)
BCE Before the Common Era (the equivalent of BC)

Distributed in the USA and Canada by
Sterling Publishing Co., Inc.
387 Park Avenue South
New York, NY 10016-8810

For information about custom editions, special sales,
premium and corporate purchases, please contact
Sterling Special Sales Department at 800-805-5489
or specialsales@sterlingpub.com.

◀◀ **Huichol yarn painting**, from Mexico, depicting
the Huichol sacred world through a range of animal,
plant and other natural motifs.

CONTENTS

Introduction 6

Part I: Place 8
Here and Now 10
Pilgrimage 13
Sacred Sites 18
Encountering Nature 21
The Elements 24
Many Directions 28
The Shamanic Otherworld 30
Spirits and Guardians 34
Altars and Shrines 36

Part II: Animal 38
Animal Brethren 40
Hunting in Shamanism 44
Encountering Animals 48
Animal Spirit Helpers 50
Animal Totems 54
Power Animals 56
Domesticated Animals 59
Mythical Creatures 62
Fur and Feather 64
Animal Rulers 66
Shapeshifting 68

Part III: Plant 72
Sacred Plants 74
Spirits in the Green 78
Meeting the Trees 80
Gathering the Harvest 84
Flowers 86
Healing Herbs 88
Incense 90

Part IV: Ritual 94
Ceremony and Ritual 96
Everyday Sacred 99
Making Offerings 102
Clothing Your Power 105
Songs of the Spirits 108
Making Music 110
Dancing Your Prayers 112
Seasonal Celebrations 116
Rites of Passage 120
Initiation 122

Part V: Spirit 124
Feeling Good in Your Skin 126
Sexuality in Shamanism 128
Dismemberment 130
Dark Shamans 134
Gaining Protection 136
Sacred Symbols 138
Power Objects 142
Divining Your Path 145
Dreaming 147
Meeting the Ancestors 152
Possession 154
Diagnosis 156
Extracting Illness 158
Soul Retrieval 160
Empowering the World 162

Conclusion 164

Notes 165
Bibliography 167
Index 172
Author Acknowledgments 175
Picture Credits 176

INTRODUCTION

There is no such thing as shamanism. This may seem like a strange thing to say at the beginning of a book about shamanism, but many researchers believe it to be true[1]. The word "shaman" comes from the Tungus word *saman* and relates to an Evenki spiritual practitioner from Siberia who makes soul journeys to the realm of the spirits on behalf of his or her community[2]. The Dutch seafarer and explorer Nicolaas Witsen, writing in the late 17th century, first adopted the word in a generalized sense, but the term is not widely used within Siberia, where different groups have (and had) different words. Nonetheless, "shaman" (an anglicized form of *saman*) is used today to describe virtually all spiritual practitioners outside mainstream religions. This has resulted in furious academic debate and even a denial that shamanism — outside an Evenki context — even exists.

Around the world there is an almost endless variety of traditional spiritual beliefs, and it can be hard to find links between them. And yet there are some. Modern research on the human brain shows that when people enter a state of trance — a usual, although not exclusive, practice of shamans — they share a broadly similar experience[3]. Cultural expectation colours the event, but the basic format is the same. The person in trance will feel as if a part of his or her body leaves to journey to an otherworldly realm inhabited by disembodied spirits, or else will feel that his or her body is possessed by another entity. In both cases, people interpret the experience as an interaction with the spirits — an almost universal aspect of shamanism. And as shamans generally live in small communities, they use the gifts such interaction brings for the benefit of others, becoming spiritual leaders, therapists and healers. The many strands of shamanism around the world thus have three main areas in common: a propensity for trance, an interaction with otherworldly spirits, and a dedication to serving the community. This is what unites traditional spiritual practitioners, wherever they may be, under the broad heading of "shamanism".

Furthermore, *you* can be part of this. If all human beings are capable of trance — which they are — it follows that we all can have a shamanic experience. You do not have to live in a traditional community, come from a lineage of spiritual elders or even have any prior religious inclination in order to follow a shamanic path; all you need is the desire to listen to the soft voices of the spirits as they call to you.

This book provides everything you need to start on your shamanic path, including practical exercises. To accompany your journeys to the otherworld, you can download drumming tracks (one continuous and one with a "callback" that signals the time to return) free at www.PrehistoricShamanism.com. To inspire you, the

▲ A Tuvan shaman (*zayran*) performs in a festival at the Kundustug mineral springs, near Kyzyl, southern Russia.

book's five parts – "Place", "Animal", "Plant", "Ritual" and "Spirit" – explain the traditions and practices of shamanic people around the world. Personal experience is paramount, so adapt rather than copy the traditional practices you feel will be helpful to you, and bear in mind that a different culture may never speak to you as profoundly as the spirits of the place where you live (or from where you originate). Remember also that shamanism is about living in tune with nature's constant ebb and flow; ultimately, you will learn this only by sitting and listening quietly to her.

Does shamanism exist? On one level it does, and yet on another it does not. People who practise what we regard as shamanism may not recognize the term or may be hostile toward it, as an assault on their individuality. Accordingly, this book uses local terms for "shaman", to capture a flavour of the differences inherent in shamanism around the world. Similarly, for ease of reading and because shamanism in many places is disappearing, practices that are historic, and may no longer exist in the same form, are described in the present tense. The bibliography includes academic studies and practical guides to help you explore further.

Can you walk the path of the spirits? Certainly you can. Shamanism will provide you with incredible power. Meeting your animal guide may be a pivotal point in your life, and learning to heal will allow you to give something back to your community. There are no rules about who can or cannot do this. If you are prepared to journey to the realm of the spirits, and to bring back some of their wisdom to help you and your community, then you are practising shamanism. The colour of your skin, your background, the culture in which you live are irrelevant. There is no preparation for shamanism, there are no exams and no qualifications; all you need to do is start. The ideal time for that is now, and the ideal place is here. Shall we begin?

PLACE

HERE AND NOW

The old monk stands deep in meditation. His body gently sways, as if catching the breeze from the mountains all around him. He smiles and his eyes open. His journey has already begun.

THE SPACE AROUND YOU

Many credit Lao Tzu, the Chinese monk who founded Taoism, with saying that every journey begins with a single step[1]. In fact, a better translation is that even the longest journey *begins where you stand*. Look around you and see where you are. Really *look*. This is your world, and you, right now, are at the centre of it. Everything you need to begin your shamanic journey is in view.

For many, home is a sanctuary where they can close the door on life's problems. There is much power in a home. In the southwest United States, Navajo (Diné) *hogans* – circular mud-brick dwellings – are models of the cosmos. The structure's three poles represent the mountains, water and corn. The entrance always faces the rising sun, and people move clockwise through the *hogan*, reflecting the sun's daily movement. Doors of prehistoric roundhouses in Britain were also aligned east. Scottish archaeology shows that people moved clockwise through a house on entering, to the living area. To move through the interior was to move through the world[2].

Recognize that your home, too, contains the world within it. When you rise, face east, then turn sunwise – clockwise – to begin your day. As you move through your home, be aware of the sun's daily journey, and recognize the sacred directions of north, east, south and west[3]. By following the natural sunwise rhythm of the world, you are moving with the flow of energy in your home. The ancient Chinese called this flow *qi* ("chi"), and arranged their living space to ensure that it was not impeded[4]. Your home may have areas where energy flows well and other places where it stagnates. By concentrating on these negative places, you may be able to free the blockage, perhaps by placing a mirror in a dark corner or by opening up a cramped space[5].

Shamans are aware of a flow of energy pervading all places. They see it as a web of life, each filament connecting every object to everything else around it.

◀◀ **The Kamikōchi mountains**, Japan, like the other great ranges of the world, provide spiritual inspiration to many.
▲ **19th-century feng shui compass**, used in China to site buildings in alignment with energy flow.

The Way of Beauty

For the Navajo people, beauty surrounds them and they
encapsulate this attitude in a prayer. It is not a comment
on the landscape, or on the objects within it, but on the
harmony and balance of all things, including the individual
giving voice to the prayer. It is an entreaty to remain
in balance, both internally and when out in the world.
Navajo spirituality is dedicated to maintaining this
balance so that all may walk in the way of beauty[6]:

With beauty before me, may I walk.
With beauty behind me, may I walk.
With beauty above me, may I walk.
With beauty below me, may I walk.
With beauty around me, may I walk.

TRADITIONAL NAVAJO PRAYER

11

This web has many names: *tapu* for the Maori people of New Zealand, *ashé* for the Santería people of Cuba and *renabti* for the Sora people of India. All recognize the web of life as the source of shamanic power. The Algonquian Indians of the eastern United States and Canada call this world-binding power *manitou*. It is the concept encapsulated in the *Star Wars* films as the "Force". As we might plug items into the electrical network, shamans can magnify their limited personal power a hundred-fold by connecting to the web of life.

TIME AND SPACE

We, too, can draw power from the web of life. Wherever you are at this moment, you can connect to it – and the time to do so is now. For the ancient Maya of Central America, time was circular, an endlessly repeating cycle of events. Time does not stretch out indefinitely, but – like a myth that is both ancient and modern – reaches back on itself. In a world that is constantly in flux there is a still centre that never moves[7]. You are at this centre and, in the words of Hawaiian shamans

▲ **Monument Valley, Utah,** homeland of the Navajo people and inspiration for their prayer that all may walk "in the Way of Beauty", a plea to maintain the harmony of all things.

(*kahuna*), "All time is now." The Amondawa people, an Amazonian tribe only discovered by the outside world in 1986, go further. They have no concept of external time, nor do they have words for "week", "month" or "year". To them, today is all there is and events are what matter. They are not controlled by time; they control time through what they do[8].

Shamans, too, work outside time. The moment they start to work, time effectively stops and they can access any moment, however distant in the past or however far in the future. Accordingly, there is no right or wrong time to start your shamanic practice.

Look around again, but this time look beyond what your eyes can see. Recognize that you are connected to everything you see and, beyond that, to everything outside your range of vision. All that you need to begin is within reach. Your journey has already begun.

PILGRIMAGE

Carrying only a digging tool, the Aboriginal youth leaves the hearth-fire and strides purposefully into the red earth of the Australian desert. With no map or compass, and no provisions for his journey, he moves over the land listening to songs of his ancestors. It is only through whispers that reach him on the wind that he will know his route is true.

SONGLINES

Australia is crossed by a network of interconnecting lines, called "songlines", a concept similar to the web of life (see pages 10 and 12). The mythical ancestors of Aboriginal people created these lines as they strode over the newly emerged land, singing everything into existence. People call this period the "Dreamtime"[1]. By learning and reciting the ancient songs, and then following the words as if they were a road-map, an Aboriginal traveller can physically travel huge distances. Along the route, every feature of the land that he or she encounters is evidence of the presence of the ancestors, and so the songlines link a trail of sacred sites. Following these lines is a pilgrimage, since the purpose of the journey is to enter sacred time and space. Aboriginal people call it "walkabout".

The intention of any pilgrimage, long or short, is to touch the sacred and to return charged and empowered by the experience[2]. The act of travelling itself becomes important and can take on an epic scale. The journey may be hazardous, literally or metaphorically – for example, to shamans of Japan a pilgrimage to the holy mountains was akin to dying and being reborn.

PREPARING FOR YOUR PILGRIMAGE

Preparation is essential, and for the shamans of the islands that stud the Pacific Ocean, this includes observing a variety of rituals and taboos that usually relate to abstaining from certain foods or sexual activity. Whether your pilgrimage is a month-long adventure or an afternoon's walk, you might like to prepare beforehand, perhaps by conducting a short ritual such as lighting a candle and stating your purpose; or you could observe a taboo, perhaps by restricting your diet before the start of your journey. Whatever you do, let it mark the transition from the mundane world into sacred reality and prepare you for the changes that may occur during your travels.

If you want to enact a pilgrimage, you first need to choose a route and a means of transport. Walking is perhaps best as it gives you time to absorb your surroundings, but you can adopt any mode of transport to suit your plans[3]. Try to link places that have significance because of their sacred nature (such as holy wells or standing stones) or because they mean something to you personally (such as the place where you were born or got

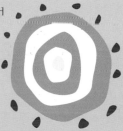

married). You could follow ley lines (prehistoric routes that link ancient sacred sites), which you can dowse using a rod or a pendant[4]. Following these lines is not unlike the way the Aborigine listens to songs of the land. In an urban environment, you could follow echoes of your past or connect locations where the natural world breaks through.

You might wish to take something with you to mark you out as a pilgrim; for example you could wear a brooch or use a specially carved staff. In medieval Europe, pilgrims to Santiago de Compostela (and then pilgrims in general) wore a scallop shell to identify themselves, and along the famous route in northern Spain images of such shells abound[5]. Reputedly, this is because pilgrims could ask for a scallop shell's scoop of food from any residence along the way.

FOLLOWING THE ROUTE

When Huichol people of Mexico set off on their annual pilgrimage to Wirikuta, a sacred desert from which their first ancestors emerged, they expect to be gone for a few weeks. Travelling on foot in times gone by, but now relying on buses for some of the way, the pilgrims stop at destinations with mythical meaning[6]. A muddy waterhole can be so sacred that novices on the pilgrimage have their eyes bound in case the place should render them blind. What the Huichol see is the beauty behind the apparent reality and their sacred connection with the web of life, which also stretches back through time and joins

them with the first ancestors. The Huichol pilgrimage has much in common with the Aboriginal walkabout, since both remove participants from this world and provide access to another, more beautiful, perfect world that only they can see. The closer Huichol people get to Wirikuta, the more the ordinary world falls away, until they find themselves in a place and time where the old myths come alive and radiate their power.

When you are travelling on your pilgrimage, try to see beyond the mundane forms of the landscape and allow the veil to lift on what lies beyond. Remember that only your body is limited to three dimensions and that your mind is free to engage with any period of the past or future. How many people have come this way over the years, leaving their footsteps before yours? If you quieten your inner voice, can you hear them pass? Look around and see what they would have seen. Might they have found that forest friendly or foreboding? Would a ford have been there instead of that busy traffic bridge? Was the bank where you stand a place where people stopped to offer their prayers for a safe crossing? You may even find that a song rises from the earth and guides you a little off your route, revealing places of wonder to those with eyes to see them.

On your pilgrimage, become aware of the web of life connecting all things around you, seen and unseen. Can you feel how you are joined to this web, especially in those locations you find particularly special? See if you can gently pull on one of the filaments that connect you to the web, drawing it into your body. Can

14

▲ **At Janai Purnima**, an annual Hindu festival in Nepal, cotton threads are tied around the wrists of pilgrims, as if connecting them to the web of life.

you feel an energy surge as you do so? This is the power of the land, filling you with energy and strength. On pilgrimage, what you give through your engagement with the sacredness of the land, you receive back through a flow of power.

ARRIVAL

Many pilgrimages end at significant places. In Burma, thousands of pilgrims travel to a small village near Mandalay called Taungbyon – a regional seat of a family of spirit Lords – where they revel in a three-day festival held in the spirits' honour[7]. In nearby Nepal, Janai Purnima is a pilgrimage in which devotees visit a sacred lake or river, first to bathe and then, as if joining themselves to the web of life, tying cotton

threads around their bodies. They hope that bathing in the water might erase sin as well as provide good fortune for the following year[8].

Mayan shamans (*chuchkajawib*) also visit sacred lakes in their Central American heartland. They go to seek benefits for the people they serve: good health, rainfall and protection from natural catastrophes. *Chuchkajawib* are able to connect to the energy that emanates from the sacred lakes, empowering themselves so they can better serve their community[9].

You might like to end your pilgrimage in an equally special place. It may be a festival site that many people visit or you may prefer a lonely sojourn in a remote and isolated location where the veil between our reality and the otherworld is thin and the source of shamanic power is strong. As we shall explore on pages 18–20, such sacred sites need approaching with care, but if you listen to the whispers on the wind, you will know that your route is true.

At Bungle Bungle Ranges in Western Australia, the Creator, Rainbow Serpent, slithered from deep underground to shape valleys and chasms with his body, reservoirs of precious water for the Kija people. Along the songlines that map the land, every natural feature is a sacred site.

SACRED SITES

The Tuvan shaman approaches the rock while drumming softly on her frame drum. The falling snow eddies around her and her chant dissipates as a soft mist in the frigid Siberian air. Reaching the lone rock in the featureless landscape of winter, she pauses, throwing her arms wide around it. She whispers her prayers and then beats her drum, drawing on the power of this sacred place.

FINDING HOLY PLACES

A sacred site might be an obvious religious centre, such as the Golden Temple of Amritsar – the most important shrine for Sikhs, where 100,000 people visit every week to offer their devotions. Similarly, Mecca in Saudi Arabia receives 13 million Muslim visitors annually, many following the Hajj pilgrimage from their native land. These are places that are universally acknowledged as sacred[1].

The Tuvan shaman (*zayran* if male and *udugen* if female), by contrast, visits sacred places known to only a few[2]. Rocks, streams and trees form the focal points of devotions, and offerings of prayer flags, tied to the branches of a tree or onto cairns of stone, are often the only signs of human visitation.

Other sites, like those the Huichol pass on their pilgrimage (see page 14), might only be visible as sacred to those who can see beyond their mundane appearance[3].

Some places may even have no physical form, such as the sacred sites dreamed by the Inca shamans (*paq'o* in their own language, although there are many grades of shaman, each with its own name) when they seek the power of their calling. Upon waking, they search for similar places in this world, making real their journeys of the night.

You might already visit places that you consider sacred and these may have formed the focal points of your pilgrimage. Or you may not yet have considered that certain places have a sacred element to which you can connect. Is there a place where you feel particularly relaxed, so that you linger there, feeling your soul restored to completeness? If so, then this is a sacred place for you, whether anyone else recognizes it as such or not.

If you can, find a sacred place close to where you live or work, so that you can easily go there whenever you feel the need for spiritual refreshment. Make any visit a pilgrimage, not necessarily through formal preparation (see page 13), but by doing just enough to ensure that a visit is an extraordinary experience.

Approach your site with reverence, acknowledging that, for you, this is a holy place set apart from the

▶ **Prayer flags at Bompori**, outside Lhasa, Tibet, mark this hill as sacred. In this region, hilltops and other landscape features are often focal points of pilgrimage and prayer.

everyday world. The Tibetan pilgrims who walked to Lhasa at the beginning of the last century prostrated themselves every few steps. Their clothes had turned to rags by the time they arrived, but their endurance ensured that this was no ordinary trip. As you draw close to your site, walk softly, taking care to place your feet gently on the earth. You may even be moved to avert your eyes in a respectful manner, refraining from talking as you approach.

Recognize your sacred site as a place where the strands of the web of life come together. Try to sense the change in atmosphere as you draw close. If you have a suitable dowsing implement (all you need is a heavy object on a string or chain, or rods[4]), hold it loosely in your hand and see what it does as you arrive at the boundary of the site. You may also discover exactly how far the power of the site reaches.

CROSSING THE BOUNDARY

Do not just stride into your sacred site, but recognize its boundaries — whether these are clear from the physical structure or landscape, or revealed to you only through the subtle energy shifts that you have dowsed. Pause at the "entrance" and seek permission before approaching further. Say who you are and state your purpose in visiting. Something, somewhere, will be listening.

You might like to walk around your site; if you do so, walk sunwise. In Tibet, pilgrims to the sacred mountain of Kailash do not set foot on the peak itself but walk around its base in reverence, asking the spirits to cleanse their sins[5]. Many pilgrims ceremonially purify themselves before entering a sacred space. For example, visitors to the Japanese landscape gardens encased in moss and mists wash their hands in a bowl of water and write out a mantra to still their mind before entering these revered places. You, too, may wish to cleanse your hands and face.

When you receive permission to enter your site – and this may arrive as a sudden gust of wind, the parting of clouds to let sunshine through or simply a feeling deep inside that approval is given – walk to the centre and spend a moment letting its energy seep into you. Like the Tuvan *udugen*, you might want to touch or even hug whatever stands before you, or you may just want to absorb the scene with your eyes, letting them linger until the energy behind the vista becomes apparent to you. Pilgrims at Varanasi, on the banks of the Ganges in India, cup water in their hands and let it pour over them in homage to their ancestors and to the gods. If there is water at your site, you could adopt a similar ceremony.

CHANNELLING POWER

Your aim is to connect not just with the site itself but also, through the myriad strands from the web of life that converge there, with all other places in the world. You followed a single strand of that web when you set out to visit the site, but there are many, many other strands, reaching far around this world and even beyond it.

Algonquian shamans of eastern North America (*wabeno*) take their energy from Venus, the Morning Star, through their dreams. The star allows them to channel its *manitou*, or energy, which the *wabeno* retain until it is released through healing or divination, the star's power enabling them to perform tasks that may be beyond normal human capability[6]. Similarly, at your sacred site use its amplified connection to the web of life to draw power into you, knowing that it will remain with you until you next need to use it. Subsume yourself in the energy of the place, letting go of anything you no longer need, and replacing it with pure energy drawn from the sacredness around you.

When you are looking for your sacred site, you may find that you are naturally drawn to places away from human habitation, but even if your site is within the bustling confines of a city, an aspect of nature probably lies at its heart. As the next pages show, a visit to a personal sacred site is the perfect time to meet nature in her true majesty. Interacting with the natural world will help you to draw on the power of your sacred place.

ENCOUNTERING NATURE

The young Ashanti makes her way unsteadily into the forbidding Ghanaian forest. Noises erupt on all sides but she remains focused on her path. Deep in the trees she stops and lets the voices of the spirits and of her ancestors emerge from the blackness and fill her with power. She will emerge changed, empowered and ready to face her destiny.

VISION QUESTS

The final stage of training for an Ashanti shaman (*akomfo*) of Ghana is a night alone in the depths of the forest. She draws her strength from the trees around her and they share her lonely ordeal. The lack of visual stimulus heightens the other senses: sounds are more intense, smells more noticeable, and the sixth sense, which allows us to see the web of life, becomes dominant. The Ashanti *akomfo*'s inner sight heightens as her outer sight diminishes[1].

In Greenland, initiates seek similar visions in caves, where they spend three days rubbing two stones together in a sunwise direction, acknowledging through this action the order of the world[2]. On the third day a spirit appears and, turning to face east, asks what the initiate seeks. A harrowing vision follows, from which initiates return as changed individuals. The stone rubbing acts in the same way as the darkness does for the Ashanti initiate – it blocks out external stimuli until the mind can focus beyond this world.

OPENING YOUR INNER EYES

Don Juan, the possibly fictitious shaman who instructed the Peruvian–American anthropologist Carlos Castaneda, asked his apprentice to sit cross-legged on the floor and to draw a circle around him, enclosing just his body[3]. Castaneda was to concentrate only on what existed inside the circle, and to ignore everything else. Predictably, he found this difficult, until he began to notice small insects crawling in the space. By observing them, he entered their world and his attention shifted from everyday reality.

Try similar focusing techniques at your sacred site. Allow your sole reality to be only what lies directly in front of you – nothing else matters. After a while, you might feel your mind shift, and you might realize that the "world" you observe holds all the secrets you seek.

Do not rely solely on your eyes. Listen to the sounds around you. Touch the earth, the rocks, the trees and anything else that lies within your domain. Smell the leaf litter – this is the scent of death and rebirth, of shamanic mystery. Taste the rain or

▶ Ashanti fertility icon (*akuaba*), dispensed by shamans in Ghana to assist conception.

21

snow; even eat the soil as you may have done as a child. Exhaustion and sensory deficit triggered the visions of the Ashanti and Greenland initiates, but, as we have seen, it is also possible to over-stimulate the mind to turn away from this world. Try both approaches.

RAIN AND SHINE

When Lakota shamans of the central plains of the United States (*wicasa wakan* if male and *winyan wakan* if female) quest for a vision during the *hanblecheyapi* ritual, they sit in a circle and do not move for four days and four nights, whatever the weather. Throughout that time, participants abstain from food and drink, and chant prayers for a revelation to appear. Extreme privation dulls their outer senses while opening up their inner sense to visions[4]. One

▲ **The Lascaux shaman** is the only human figure among the many paintings at this 17,000-year-old French site; he is believed to be in trance, his staff and bird-totem at his side.

wicasa wakan, Little Wound, related that his shamanic knowledge came from a vision of the wind.

When visiting your sacred site, try to do so in all weathers. This is a great way of experiencing nature in all her moods, not just those that are pleasant or benign. Little Wound's vision of the wind was unlikely to have been inspired by a mere breeze, and many shamans draw their energy from the apparent violence of lightning. Nature is raw, unpredictable and full of power. By connecting with her tempestuous forms, our attention is subsumed far more thoroughly than on a fine, sunny day. Remember the Navajo teaching that beauty occurs in balance (see page 11). As our outer senses dull through the buffeting or soaking we receive, so our inner senses open.

PAINTED ROCKS

The Lakota seek their visions on mountains that have been sacred to the tribe for generations, the spirits drawing close as soon as a seeker appears. Murut shamans of highland Borneo also desire visions, and might ascend hills to meet the spirits or else spend the night in a graveyard waiting for dead ancestors to appear[5]. One way of commemorating the experience is to leave an image of the vision painted or engraved on rock. Some of the earliest art in the world, painted on cave walls in southern France and northern Spain, very likely reflects the visions of Ice Age shamans[6]. Elsewhere, there may be particular dates or times of day when the meaning of the rock art is revealed by sunlight. Every winter solstice at La Rumorosa in northern Mexico, for example, the light of the rising sun forms a dagger that crosses the eyes of a rock painting of an antlered shaman, making it flare into life[7]. The glare of the sun may have blinded the shaman on the rock, but it also opened his or her eyes to deeper mysteries.

All these places are suitable for you to quest for your own vision, searching for the help and inspiration you need. You will journey out of this world and into another, before returning changed, empowered and ready to face your destiny.

QUEST FOR A VISION

• •

Follow these steps whenever you visit a sacred site in search of a vision.

1. Leave this world behind by journeying to your site on pilgrimage. This is a special journey, so make sure you prepare for it spiritually beforehand.

2. When you arrive, speak your name and intention at whatever you perceive to be the "entrance" to the site and wait for a response before continuing.

3. Make yourself comfortable and still your mind, either through inwardly meditating or else by concentrating intensely on the miniature world at your feet.

4. Continue stilling your mind, until you touch, however briefly, a realm outside this reality where visions arise and power flows.

5. Finally, you need to return — not just physically but also mentally. Give thanks for whatever you have received and then resume your ordinary existence, retaining the power and inspiration you have gained.

THE ELEMENTS

Stones blaze white-hot in the heart of the fire; people take long poles and spread them out to form a wide platform. The heat is intense and many shield their eyes from the glare. Suddenly, the shaman appears, calling in the native language of Fiji for protection from the spirits. The shaman leaps onto the glowing stones and proceeds to dance, drawing power from the element they embody.

HANDLING FIRE

In many communities, mastery of fire is a sign of shamanic calling. Fijian shamans would not expect to burn while performing a ceremony dancing on white-hot stones. Similarly, Ojibwa shamans (*jiisakiiwinini*) from the northeastern United States, handle burning hot coals without harm, and Zuni spiritual practitioners in the far southwest even swallow them. These are outward demonstrations of an inner mastery, through which the shaman controls and absorbs the power of fire and, rather than being burned, stores it in his or her body for later release[1]. This is the same technique you used to absorb power from your sacred site (see page 20). Aboriginal shamans describe filaments emerging from the flames, which they can use to send the fire into something else or even travel along.

Retaining fire within the body is especially important in colder climates, where shamans have considerable resilience to freezing temperatures[2].

Manchu shamans in northeastern China endure initiation rites that require them to swim beneath the frozen sea with only their inner fire keeping them alive. Inuit shamans (*angakkuq*) prove their mastery of fire by drying frozen sheets of paper on their bodies. One element (fire) counters the effects of another (water, present as ice).

ELEMENTAL CONNECTION

Fire, water, earth and air are the traditional Western elements. They arise from ancient Babylonian tradition, recorded in the epic poem *Enûma Eliš* some 1,600 years ago. People believed that everything in existence broke down into four constituent forms, called elements. Ancient Egyptians also recognized four elements, and the Goddess Isis stated that every person embodies one or other of them[3]. Attributing passion to fire, emotion to water, intellect to air and bodily sensation to earth still seems to make sense and it is interesting to reflect on how you manifest each element – although nobody is likely to embody a single element alone.

Understanding your composition allows you to determine any elemental lack. You may already have

▶ **Waterfalls at Nagano**, Japan, offer a dramatic experience of the element of water. Japanese shamans stand under waterfalls for days, drawing on their inner fire to survive.

24

experienced the elements at your sacred site, especially if you visited it in a variety of weathers, but you can also plan special pilgrimages to experience each element in turn. Plenty of caves are open to the public and these provide an incredible sensation of being within the body of the earth. Climbing a mountain is a wonderful way of connecting to air, and a visit to the coast allows communion with water. Fire is present all year round through the rays of the sun, or you might want to connect to it by lighting a bonfire or attending a fireworks display. Try to feel the connection with each element's core and draw its energy into you. This might be easy with earth or water, but fire and air are ephemeral and more difficult to reach. This may be why mastery of fire, the most fleeting element of all, is so highly prized by shamans.

Japanese shamans, who are usually women, use their mastery of inner fire to endure standing under intensely cold waterfalls for days at a time. As with vision quests, a feat of physical endurance shifts the individual's awareness away from the mundane world and toward the inner realm of the shaman. And exposure to one element brings mastery over another[4]. You do not necessarily need to stand under a freezing shower, but try to connect to water as you wash your body, and draw something of its power into you. The shamans of northern Eurasia hold water to be sacred and use their immersion in the element as an opportunity to heal and restore their power. They consider bathrooms as sacred spaces that allow direct connection with water, and many rituals occur in this most unlikely place.

In West Africa, an entire religion has developed around Mami Wata, the local, pidgin name for "Mother Water"[5]. This deity inhabits all bodies of water, and her devotees, who live along the coast of the region, perform ceremonies of healing, purification and sacrifice in her honour. Mami Wata devotees draw their power from the water and retain it within their bodies, just as others draw upon the power of fire.

Your sacred site will definitely contain earth, air and the fire of the sun, but it might not contain water. Shamans consider places where all four elements come together as particularly powerful. If there is no water at your site, you might like to take some in a bottle or a bowl next time you visit. You may find that the

▲ **Fire and air** are prominent at this reserve in California, as sunlight slashes through lofty redwoods. Visiting places that embody certain elements can be a source of healing.

addition of the final element of the four changes the atmosphere and energy of the place.

The Lakota people of central United States bring all four elements together during their *inipi* or sweat lodge ceremony[6]. Participants sit huddled on the earth in a small, domed tent. Hot rocks heat the air intensely and water splashed onto the rocks produces steam, causing almost overwhelming heat in the near total darkness, mirroring other feats of shamanic endurance. Evidence of similar lodges occurs across prehistoric Europe and they are still used by the Nenets of northwestern Siberia[7].

THE FIFTH ELEMENT

Hindus and Buddhists add a fifth element to earth, fire, air and water, which is sometimes also adopted by the neo-shamanic movement in the Western world: ether or spirit. This fifth element seems especially suited to shamanism in which, as we will see, every object contains spirit at its heart. The Japanese also credit this fifth element as being the source of creativity.

The Dagara of Ghana recognize earth, fire, water, mineral and nature as their five elements, whereas the Chinese divide the world into wood, fire, earth, metal and water[8]. The Chinese classification further emphasizes the connections between each element and considers them to be in a constant state of flux, each moving from one state to another. Depending on the sequence of change, this can be either a process of creating or of destroying. Each element has the power to do harm as well as to heal.

You might want to formulate your own system of elements that best describes your world. Adding wood and metal to the four traditional elements might better reflect the objects that surround you, and you could even add the "element" of plastic. Modern science recognizes 118 chemical elements in its Periodic Table.

Dividing the world into constituent parts seems innate to human thought, from the elements to the concept of direction (see pages 28–9). Finding the essential nature of objects allows us to understand them, and to draw power from the element they embody.

27

MANY DIRECTIONS

· ·

The Mongolian woman emerges from her round felt tent and salutes the rising sun. Using a holed ladle, she scoops some of the first milk she took from the bleating flock of sheep just before dawn and flicks a generous spray to each side of her, then in front, then behind. She flicks more toward the sky and down toward the earth, entreating the spirits of these places to protect and watch over her.

PATH OF THE SUN

Mongolian people divide the earth into four directions, centred on the place where they stand[1] – another reminder that all we need lies right here. The directions are those recognized by people the world over and far back into the past: north, south, east and west.

These cardinal directions are connected to the daily journey of the sun across the sky, and the way in which the sun's position on the horizon varies over the year. Taking all our examples from the northern hemisphere, the summer solstice marks the sun's most northerly point and the winter solstice its most southerly point. Falling between these are the two equinoxes, when the sun rises from a point exactly due east and sets exactly due west. These dates are also remarkable because only then are the lengths of day and night in perfect balance. Thus, we have our first two directions. The sun ascends to its highest point in the sky exactly due south and, continuing the trajectory, it reaches its (unseen) lowest point in the night exactly due north. We now have our four directions, arising from the apparent path of the sun.

Prehistoric people set up monuments such as Stonehenge in England to reflect the sun's changing position[2]. Today, people are commemorating once more the movements of the sun. For example, at the end of May and beginning of July, the rising and setting sun aligns with the grid of the Manhattan streets, and is cause for celebration in New York.

CHARACTERIZING THE DIRECTIONS

The Maya undertake pilgrimages to the four directions, visiting sacred lakes and mountains that lie north, south, east and west of where they start. In many cultures each direction is considered an entity in its own right, each with its specific character, power and influence. In modern Druidry, to call upon the north is to invoke Bear; to call upon the east is to invoke Hawk; to call upon the south is to invoke Stag; and to call upon the west is to invoke Salmon. The Hopi people of the southwestern United States also assign animals to each of the four directions, placing Bear in the west and changing Hawk to Eagle in the east[3]. Buryat shamans divide deities between east and west, with the benevolent in the west and the malign in the east.

We can allocate elements to each direction, with earth in the north, fire in the south, air in the east and

28

MEDICINE WHEELS

Native American tribes laid out huge spoked wheels of stone on the ground. They called these "medicine wheels", medicine in this context meaning holy rather than healing. One of the best preserved is at Big Horn in Wyoming (use of this site may date back 7,000 years). The wheel's 28 spokes could relate to the days of a lunar month, but their exact meaning is unknown. Perhaps the convergence of many directions mirrored the convergence of people into one universal group. It is striking that all tribes observed Big Horn as a neutral meeting place and camped there in peace[4].

Medicine wheels remind us that although there are traditionally four directions, we may also honour others[5]. Mongolian women, as we have seen, greet the day by offering milk to the six directions (including up to the sky and down to the earth), while the Dagara of Ghana emphasize that these six directions are all relative to where we begin.

water in the west. We can also assign times of year, starting with spring in the east and ending with winter in the north. We can even use the stages of human life, starting with birth in the east. Encompassing each stage of life in a cyclical pattern is a reminder of the shamanic adage that time is not linear but circular.

HARNESSING POWER

At your sacred site, or even within your home, ascertain which direction is which, by observing the sun in the sky or by using a magnetic compass. Stand facing each direction in turn and try to discern the difference in energy that emanates from there. Are you drawn to any particular direction? If so, can you emulate the Maya shamans and devise a pilgrimage to journey that way?

You might also like to follow the Mongolian woman described opposite and start each day by greeting the directions. If you do so, start in the east with the rising sun. You might see each direction as personified by an animal or even a deity, and this may help you to integrate its associated power. As you have done before, feel a tangible connection with every direction you face, absorbing some of its power into your body. Think of the medicine wheel (see box, above) with its spokes leading away from the centre[6]. You are now standing at that centre and the spokes are lines of power leading to you. Add the sky above and the earth below so that power surrounds you entirely; remember also the Navajo words about beauty being both above and below you (see page 11). In fact, an adaptation of that prayer would form an appropriate ritual to start the day.

There is one further direction and that is to move within. Before you do this, call upon the six directions that radiate out from the place you inhabit, entreating their spirits to protect and watch over you.

THE SHAMANIC OTHERWORLD

The shaman sits quite still, her back resting against the trunk of a favourite tree, her portable music player set to loud, repetitive drumming. Her awareness shifts inward. Imagining herself crawling inside the tree, she follows its route deep into the ground. A tunnel opens before her and she follows it down, deeper and deeper, until at last she steps out into another world. She knows this place well and her steps through this incredible realm are sure.

ENTERING TRANCE

In addition to the six (or more) directions of this world, there is another route that shamans travel, and that is to leave this world and journey to another. It is an inner journey, seemingly contained entirely within the mind, but to shamans the world over, the otherworld that they reach is a very real place[1].

Entry to the otherworld is achieved via trance, which, for many in the Western world, is a challenging, even threatening, state that is alien to normal life[2]. This is an entirely mistaken view. Everyone dreams at night – this is the most common form of trance.

▶ *Incaic Vision*, a painting by Peruvian healer Pablo Amaringo, depicts a shamanic trance, the shamans appearing dressed as Incas.

30

Shamanic journeying is similar to dreaming but more controlled, and certainly no more dangerous or alien. Almost all traditional people in the world today experience trance and it is an important part of our prehistoric heritage[3]. Humans evolved to enter trance.

The key to trance is to shift awareness away from this world to the inner realm. We have seen how some people achieve this through sensory deprivation and other hardships while they vision-quest. Another route is through ingesting psychoactive plants. However, by far the simplest method is to listen to repetitive drumbeats, which slow the brainwave cycle and enable anyone to experience trance in a safe and controlled manner[4]. Shamans from Siberia to Haiti and from South Africa to the Arctic use drumming in this way. Western shamans have also adopted this method, by listening to a recording on a portable music player, like the shaman on page 30.

There are many ways of reaching the otherworld while in trance, but following a long and winding tunnel is among the most common. In Siberia, shamans often describe the entrance to the tunnel as being at the base of a tree and only visible to the person in trance. Across much of northern Eurasia, shamans recognize certain landforms, such as caves and north-flowing rivers, as being portals between the worlds, and in Japan people believe that certain mountains give access to the otherworld[5].

Scientists think that people in trance hallucinate and that this accounts for the visions they experience[6]. To shamans this is nonsense – the visions are real. They explain the journey to the otherworld as a form of spirit travel in which the soul of the shaman leaves his or her body and travels independently from it.

OTHERWORLD LANDSCAPES

The form of the otherworld visited will vary from person to person. Black Elk, a Lakota *wicasa wakan*, commented that the inner landscape will always relate to the outer landscape[7]. Within the otherworld, you may find forests, rivers, deserts, mountains and all the other geographical features with which you are familiar. For many shamans, the otherworld is a reversal of this world. Coast Salish shamans of the northwestern seaboard of North America make their most important journeys to the otherworld at midnight in winter so that in the alternative realm it will be a summer's day[8]. The landscape may have an ethereal, even transient quality, but it is quite real; the Shuar shamans (*payé*) of the Amazon forests of Ecuador and Peru consider our world to be merely an illusion of the otherworld, which is the true reality.

Most shamans agree that the otherworld divides into three: an upperworld and a lowerworld, with a middleworld between them. We live in the middleworld, which also can be viewed with shamanic vision, as you have already started to do when observing the web of life. Trance will increase this ability and also allow you, or your soul, to move through time and space without your physical body. The otherworld is vast. Many shamans believe there are many layers stacked above and beneath the middleworld. Shamans from Niger (*zimas*) believe there are seven layers of upperworld and seven of lowerworld, and shamans of Borneo agree. The Teleutian shamans of western Siberia believe there are sixteen layers in all: six above and nine below the middleworld. It seems that every shamanic community has a sightly different belief in this regard[9].

The journey to the otherworld mirrors pilgrimage in this world and requires similar preparation and care. Your intention is important, in the same way that you set out on pilgrimage with a particular purpose in mind. Initially it is perfectly acceptable to have the intention just to look around and explore[10].

We have seen that many shamans follow a tunnel to the lowerworld, but this is less effective in reaching the upperworld. In Nepal, a shaman climbs a tree and then pushes off its highest branches. In Korea shamans ascend a ladder; and Carib shamans from Central America climb up a twisted rope. You can adopt any of these routes or come up with your own. The key for reaching the upperworld is to keep rising until you pass a clear interface between the worlds.

The exercise on this page will help you to reach the otherworld, whether you go to the upper- or lowerworld or remain here in the middleworld[11]. Exploring this strange domain, you may notice some of its denizens. By familiarizing yourself with the landscape, you will ensure that, when you come to meet these entities, your steps through this incredible realm will be sure.

JOURNEY TO THE OTHERWORLD

Many people find the sound of repetitive drumming helps them to enter a trance state and reach the otherworld.

1. Start your "callback" drumming download (see page 6). As you close your eyes and quieten your mind, letting this world fall away, state the intention of your journey. For the first few times, use: "I am journeying to the otherworld to explore and look around."

2. Imagine entering a hole with a tunnel leading into the ground. (Later, you can imagine pushing off the top branches of a tree to the upperworld or imagine getting up and moving around to explore the middleworld.)

3. Move along the tunnel. After a while, notice a light at its end. Go toward it and emerge into the otherworld.

4. Take your time to look around, maybe walking a little distance to get your bearings.

5. When you hear the drumming stop and a faster rhythm begin, finish your exploration and return to the tunnel. The increased tempo will help you to move quickly back along it.

6. As you step out of the tunnel, become aware of being back in your physical body. Then open your eyes.

33

SPIRITS AND GUARDIANS

The Inuit shaman has left his body far behind and now stands on an ice flow in the otherworld. He repeats the intention of his journey: "I want to know if the hunting weather will hold." An enormous black bird flaps lazily down. In its rough caw, it says, "A storm is coming; there will be no hunting today." The shaman thanks his spirit guide for its help, recognizing its presence as the source of his shamanic power.

HOME OF SPIRITS

When you journey to the otherworld, you may see various spirits who live there. Most will ignore you unless you approach them. Some may be antagonistic, but others will take you under their protection. To the Inuit *angakkuq* above, the black bird was an old and trusted friend, whose advice he relied upon. Inuit artist Tudlik captured precisely this moment in his famous stone-cut print entitled *Bird Dream Forewarning Blizzard*, created in 1959[1]. To the *angakkuq*, everything in this world has a spirit that can be approached in the otherworld, from animals to landscape features and even intangible forms such as weather or emotions[2]. The Chukchi people, inhabiting the far northwestern arctic region of Siberia, say: "All that exists, lives."[3] To them, and to most other shamanic communities, everything is alive and has a spirit.

Just as you can visit the spirits' home, so they can cross into our realm. The Amazonian Shuar believe that when a *payé* calls upon the help of an object's spirit, it leaves the object and meets the *payé* in the otherworld[4]. As a spirit has many and varied forms – which do not always bear any relation to the physical object it represents – the spirit will adopt a form that the *payé* will recognize. When you journey to meet a spirit, be prepared for it not to appear as you expect. The spirit of a rock may appear as a bird, for example.

SPIRIT GUIDES

Everyone has one or more spirit guides in the otherworld, and all it takes to connect with them is to journey with the intention of meeting up. When you arrive in the otherworld, move around as usual but pay particular attention to spirits. If you see one several times, or if it approaches you, ask if it is your spirit guide. If it replies in the affirmative, spend time getting to know it. Your guide may take many forms, so trust that whatever appears to you is exactly right at this time. Often such guides can be animals or even deceased ancestors. Ask the spirit for guidance and for new insights into your life. Try journeying to meet your spirit guide with specific problems, changing your intention to reflect whatever you need. Your intention will determine the help you receive.

▶ *Bird Dream Forewarning Blizzards*, by Tudlik (1959), depicts the visitation of an Inuit spirit guide.

SPIRITS OF PLACE

You might also like to meet the spirit of your sacred site or the spirit of your home. Such spirits of place both represent and are contained within the land, and watch over it rather than over individuals. Remember to change your intention before journeying to the otherworld to meet them. Meeting spirits of place is easier at the sites they inhabit, although it is not always necessary to be there. If you have been regularly visiting your sacred site, its spirit has probably already noticed you. As with all spirits, a spirit of place can take many forms, so ask its identity if you are in doubt.

The Tuvan *udugen* we saw honouring her sacred site (see page 18) was probably chanting her welcome to its spirit. Once you have befriended the spirit of your

sacred site, you can do the same. The Semai shamans of Borneo (*pawing*) also revere the spirits of their sacred places. The highest-ranking *pawing* are those who interact with guardians of the land, harnessing power directly from the landscape[5]. You can do the same if you meet the spirit of your home, asking it to protect you and your family.

When spirits of place change location, they often assume a different guise. The spirits of New Orleans Voudou shamanism are different to those of their heartland in Haiti, which are also very different from the spirits of West Africa from which they emerged[6]. However, some spirits of place seem tethered to one location. Australian Aboriginals have helping spirits associated with trees known as *minggah*, a word meaning "spirit-tree"[7]. The health of the spirit depends on the health of the tree — a reminder that spirits of place suffer when their domain is damaged.

Meet a variety of spirits, calling first for your spirit guide to keep you from harm. (Occasionally we need a guide's protection from some of the entities that abide in the otherworld.) As the next pages describe, you can dedicate a small area to honouring your guide in this world, rather as the Tuvan *udugen* did at her lone rock — a natural altar. Know that your guide will always be there for you, watching over you and answering your questions. Over time, you will recognize its presence as the source of your shamanic power.

35

ALTARS AND SHRINES

• •

High in the Andes, the shaman spreads out his cloth bundle on the ground. He divides the brightly coloured material into three areas where he will lay his tools, reflecting the three worlds through which he walks. Stones mark the four directions, and swords offer protection. Bowls of earth, animal parts and plants reflect the powers he will call upon. A crucifix and picture of the Virgin complete the altar. It is a symbol of the world and of the shaman's power.

SACRED OBJECTS

The Andean altar (*mesa*) is a bundle of sacred objects that the *paq'o* arranges before conducting a ritual. The placement is ordered by the three realms of the otherworld and the four directions of this world[1]. As the layout of Navajo houses reflects all existence (see page 10), so the entire world lies on the *mesa*. Tamang shamans (*bompo*) of Nepal place a candle at the centre of their altars to symbolize the sun. For them, the altar represents the heavens as well as the Earth[2].

Many of the objects on the Andean *mesa* originate from sacred places and contain something of the spirits of those places. There may be an object from your sacred site that you can collect and invite the spirit of the site to enter. Holding the object, journey to meet the spirit and ask it to imbue your object with its power. The item will provide a direct connection to your sacred site and its spirit. In Australia, tourists chipping pieces off Uluru, the huge rock sacred to the Pitjantjatjara Aborigines, were reminded that their souvenirs contained the uprooted and angry spirit of Uluru[3]. People who took these chippings reported bad luck, and some mailed their malevolent souvenirs back to the tribe. Always ask permission from the spirit of place before collecting anything from your sacred site.

CREATING AN ALTAR OR SHRINE

To house the object that contains the essence of your sacred site, you could create an altar. This can be portable, like the *mesa*, or a table-top or shelf in your home. Try to reflect the world in your altar, perhaps by aligning it to the directions or by including symbols of the elements. As you gather shamanic objects and tools, you can place them on your altar, so that it becomes a concentrated focus of your shamanic power[4].

Nähñu shamans of Mexico perform most of their shamanic work by the side of their altars. If they have to work away from home, they replicate the altar, even on a mountain peak or deep in a cave[5]. Subtle changes to the altar reflect the task the shaman is undertaking (even the simple Andean *mesa* changes depending on the spirits the *paq'o* wishes to call upon).

Nähñu shamans use a candle on their altars to call their spirit guides. Depending on the flame's strength and direction, a spirit can give advice without the

shaman entering trance. The candle also provides a light to protect the shaman's physical body during the otherworld journey. Many Western shamans also like to light a candle before they enter the otherworld.

Rai shamans of eastern Nepal (known in their own languages as *makpa*, *sele mop* or *seleme*) have altars with power objects that form a direct link to the otherworld, a bridge that the spirits use to cross to this world[6]. Hmong shamans (*txiv neeb*) of Thailand and Laos (with a large community in the southeastern United States), leave a path clear for the spirits between the door of the home and the altar room[7]. You should consider similar lines of access for the spirits and the energy they bring. When energy cannot flow freely, it stagnates and turns negative (see page 10).

More permanent than an altar, a shrine is a home for particular spirits and a place the shaman can always go to interact with them. Anthropologists in Zambia recorded a Ndembu shaman (*ayimbuki*) constructing a shrine from a forked stick with a stone at its base. Painting the shrine and his body with white clay, the *ayimbuki* called for success in the hunt. Whenever he

▲ **Uluru in Central Australia** is imbued with its spirit's power; it is said that tourists removing chippings as souvenirs have subsequently been dogged with bad luck.

caught prey, he smeared the shrine with blood and placed the animal's head on it. The shrine was a means through which he called on his spirit guides and a resting place for the spirits of the animals he caught[8].

You could construct a shrine in a corner of your home, or outside, by a tree or a rock. Invite a spirit to inhabit the place by adopting the technique you used to empower an object from your sacred site. Whether the spirit makes your shrine its permanent home, or whether it simply leaves something of its energy there, does not matter. Every time you approach your shrine, you will feel the spirit draw close. In Buddhist Thailand, people still honour the spirits, providing them with shrines and food, and seeking their advice[9].

Reflecting your sacred site, the shaman's three worlds and the directions, elements and spirits, your altar or shrine manifests all you have learned so far and is a symbol of the world and of your shamanic power.

ANIMAL BRETHREN

Great Spirit called together all the Animal People and told them that other beings were coming among them – people who walked upright on two legs. The Animal People were excited and asked what they should do to prepare. Great Spirit thought and told them that the new people would want all the Animal People to have names, so that they might recognize each animal. The Animal People did not understand why this was necessary, but agreed to the names Great Spirit gave them. It was to change everything.

KINSHIP

The story above is from the Coast Salish people of the northwestern seaboard of North America, but it reflects a widely held Native American belief that before humans arrived on Earth animals held sway. Many Native Americans still use the term "Animal People", and each animal, as Great Spirit named it, has an origin story that has been told and retold across generations. These stories define the relationship between people and particular animals[1]. In some communities, such as the Crow – a tribe who lived along the Yellowstone River Valley before being forcibly settled on reservations in Montana – a shaman (*akbaalía*) has a spirit parent who may be an animal

◀◀ **Coyote** is a trickster spirit who likes to cause chaos and may hinder as much as he helps.

such as an elk, an eagle or a buffalo[2]. Similarly, Hopi people of the southwestern United States refer to their animal spirit guides as "Father"[3]. The relationship between traditional peoples and animals is profound, with an intimacy that is missing in our modern world.

For indigenous people of Karelia in northern Russia, the bear is semi-divine. In reverence, people never speak its true name; instead, they use nicknames, such as "Older Brother", suggesting kinship. In Finland, the Skolt Sámi believe they are descended from the union of a girl and a bear, so every individual is distantly related to the animal[4]. Many rituals and taboos recognize and honour this connection, especially when people hunt bears for food.

There is a deep truth in these ancient myths: we are all descended from animals and, at one time, only animals walked the Earth. Parts of the human brain, such as the hippocampal-septal region, are ancient in evolutionary terms and these older areas of the brain show the most activity when shamans are in trance. Shamanism arose very early in our evolution, possibly when we were still more animal than human. This may explain why much of shamanism has an instinctive and innate quality that makes it feel natural to practise[5].

RESPECT

The modern world has divorced us from our animal roots and from animals in general. Apart from a very few species that we share our lives with (and force to adapt to our lifestyles), most animals are either wild or a source of food[6]. We have lost the visceral connection to animals as older and wiser brethren. Animals had qualities that humans once sought to emulate. Now, to be called an animal is an insult.

In West Africa, people consider certain animals to have angry spirits that will haunt individuals who have unjustly preyed on their kind. Perhaps it is a reflection of today's world that people believe these animals have risen against them and seek to do them harm. Shamans try to restore the balance. In the Kalahari Desert of central Africa, !Kung shamans (*n/um k"auʌi*) teach the older tradition that animals were once people and deserve our respect. *N/um k"auʌi* interpret animal rules and show how people can adopt animals as models for their own lives. Many of the myths concerning individual creatures show animals to be wise teachers, helping their younger human brethren to find their feet in the world[7].

Even in the West, we may conclude that animals attune more readily than we do to the unseen forces of the world such as the web of life and the presence and power of spirits. It is possible that what we observe during shamanic trance, animals see all the time. For them, spirits are just part of normal existence.

Shamans often interact with animal spirits when they meet them in the otherworld. Freed from the constraints of their animal form in this reality, such spirits are a source of incredible wisdom and power[8]. Your own spirit guide may well have appeared in the form of an animal.

Spend some time considering your relationship with animals. You might share your life with a beloved pet and he or she may have taught you many things over the years, not least of which is the value of unconditional love (animals can love with humbling depth). But are there also wild animals in your life, even if only the birds on the windowsill of your inner-city flat? Do these animals have anything to teach you? Consider the ambiguity of your relationship with animals, especially if you eat meat, wear leather or own products originating from animals. Traditional people, including shamans, kill and eat animals to survive, and often these are the same animals they revere as kin. The Sámi, who consider themselves descended from a bear, still hunt and eat its flesh. No matter how much they honour the remains, they have still taken the life of the creature. This ambiguity between reverence for the spirit and dependence on the flesh is not something shamanism ignores or pretends is otherwise, and we will consider this on pages 44–7. Naming animals was the start, and wild creatures moved from being Animal People to being characterized by different qualities. Over time, this was to change everything.

41

From animals we can learn a more natural and uninhibited way of interacting with the world. Animals live in the moment and are true to their thoughts and feelings. Ancient people admired and revered animals and knew they could gain much from observing them, just as we can today.

HUNTING IN SHAMANISM

The Sámi hunting party has been successful, as the shaman predicted it would be, finding Honey Paws deep in the taiga forest. Every hunter jabbed his spear into the flesh so that no one knows who struck the fatal blow. Immediately afterwards, the hunters drop to their knees and beg forgiveness, promising the bear they will honour him in death with songs and a joyous welcome from the women of the community. They promise that none of his bones will break and that they will bury him in the ground, ready to rise again next spring. To kill an animal is not to bring death, but to hasten rebirth and new life.

PERMISSION TO KILL

The Sámi bear hunt is an elaborate process with myriad taboos honouring the creature's spirit[1]. Respect for the prey is paramount, from asking permission from the spirit of the animal before the hunt begins, to burying the bones in an anatomically correct sequence so that the bear may live again the following spring. This is not a convenient means of assuaging guilt, but an involved and time-consuming process that lasts for

River Fishing, by the Canadian Inuit artist Victor Ekootak (1966), shows a community spearing fish caught in a stone trap.

44

many months. For an entire year following the hunt, no woman is allowed to travel in the sled in which the bear's body rode, for fear of sterility.

The Sámi need to bridge the ambiguity between revering the bear – the creature from which they think they are descended – and killing it for food. As the Danish explorer Knud Rasmussen noted when he spent time with the Inuit of Greenland, human food consists mainly of animal souls, putting those who consume them in great peril[2]. *Angakkuq* journey to animals for help and advice, but hunters journey to the same animals to kill them and feed on their flesh. These two conflicting demands have to be reconciled.

!Kung *n/um k"ausi* of the Kalahari Desert sing songs about animals the night before a big hunt[3]. Entering trance, they visit the animal spirits and ask permission to kill some of their kind. If permission is forthcoming, the spirits indicate where hunters will find game. In this way, the prey acquiesces and accepts its fate. If it did not, the people would starve.

RELIANCE AND RESPECT

In the Western world, many people choose not to eat meat. Wearing fur is

▶ *Shaman with Spear and Knife*, by Inuit artist David Ikuutaq (1979), depicts a shaman in the form of a walrus.

widely considered unacceptable, but wearing leather arouses less passion. Testing cosmetics on animals is condemned, while undertaking medical research on those same animals is tolerated. Many people, perhaps most, do not consider the wider implications of our reliance on animals for human health and prefer to avoid the hard ethical questions this generates. To traditional shamans, this attitude would be incomprehensible. While they would readily accept our use of animals for food, clothing and medicine, our indifference to their spiritual fate and our double standards regarding the treatment of pets versus that of factory-farmed animals would bemuse them. Traditional people do not avoid these issues[4].

Inuit people consider all dead animals potentially dangerous. Polar bears demand particular attention, and their souls are bestowed with many gifts as they depart to the afterlife. No Inuit allows a dog to chew on the bones of hunted animals, lest the soul be offended. Many Native American people return bones to the point where the animal met its death so that the soul may be reborn, providing more game for people to hunt in the future. For example, the Naskapi of Quebec in Canada take the bones of beavers back to the wetlands, and the Plateau peoples of western North America place salmon bones back in the river where the fish was caught[5]. In an age where sustainability is increasingly important, this approach has much to teach us about stepping lightly on the Earth and showing respect to all creatures.

In the Western world, meat and leather are commodities that we buy, use and discard without a second thought – we are far removed from the reality involved in butchering and in the preparation of products derived from animals. Traditional shamans would not say it was wrong to eat meat or use leather, but they would say it was wrong to do so with no concern for the creature's welfare or the destination of its soul. When Evenki people of eastern Siberia sacrifice and then consume animals during rituals, shamans care for the souls so that each animal can safely reach the afterlife. This ensures that the animals will not withhold game from the hunters[6]. The least we can do for the animals that we eat, wear or rely upon for our medical well-being is to offer them thanks. You could also journey to the spirits of these animals, asking if there is anything else you can do to honour their gifts, thereby restoring the ancient balance between the Human People and the Animal People.

SOUL EXCHANGE

In Siberia, people maintain balance by offering their own souls in return for all the animal souls they have taken in the hunt. Just as humans live on the flesh and energy of animals, so animal souls live on the flesh and energy of humans. As people kill and consume more animal energy, animal souls consume more human energy and this is why people grow old and die. Human death, when it comes, is the ultimate payback, not just for the animals the person has killed during his or her lifetime but also for all those animals his or her descendants will kill in the future. Mutual consumption of energy brings death to humans and animals alike in an endless cycle of reciprocity[7].

Many shamans journey to the animal spirits to bargain on behalf of the community, trying to reduce the amount of energy demanded from humans, while maximizing the number of animals killed in the hunt. The Evenki may even sacrifice members of the community in return for more game, by shooting arrows at people's dwellings – the nearer an arrow lands to the house, the more likely it is that the person living there will soon die. Individual lives are traded so that the community may live[8]. A (male) shaman may marry an animal spirit and perform the duties of husband, arranging the exchange of human souls for animal energy. The institution of marriage sets the terms and obligations of such arrangements. The shaman himself is unable to eat the meat of the species of animal he marries, as to do so would be incestuous.

Consider your relationship with animals and how you can re-establish the reciprocity and respect that traditional people take for granted. Taking and consuming animal life is a form of power transfer – animal to human. But how can we give something back? Our focus should not be to bring death, but always to hasten rebirth and bring new life.

ENCOUNTERING ANIMALS

The Huichol shaman snatches up the bearded lizard from its desert home, in the heartlands of Mexico. Avoiding its venomous fangs, the shaman thanks the animal for giving itself to him, then nips the end off its tail with his knife. The lizard scurries away as the shaman wipes the blood onto his face, throat, wrists and feet. He is now bound to the animal through blood and he will keep the tail tip as a power object. The shaman voices his thanks again, for he recognizes that no animal encounter is ever coincidental.

ANIMALS ON THE PATH

The Huichol shaman (*mara'akame*) repeats this ritual with several other bearded lizards, or with horned toads or wiexu snakes, to develop a deep connection with each creature[1]. Once the ritual is over, he leaves offerings to the animals at an outdoor shrine. He believes each animal appears willingly and acquiesces in the procedure, offering its help for the future.

To Sámi people, an encounter with any wild animal is potentially dangerous, as the animal has crossed from its domain into the realm of humans. People proceed with caution until they establish the animal's motivation. Across the taiga forest of Siberia, encountering a bear in winter – when most are hibernating – is an ill-omen and the creature may even be a dark shaman[3]. Half a world away, in southern Chile, Mapuche people adopt a similar approach to animals out of their natural habitat. *Wekufe* are malevolent forces that the shaman (*machi*) constantly guards her community against (most shamans are women). *Wekufe* often appear as animals, especially those that seem out of place or combine two animal forms in one[4].

Other people revere animals that appear outside their natural habitat. The ancient Scythians, a nomadic tribe of the Eurasian steppe, decorated objects with images of a variety of animals from far-off mountains. Perhaps these alien animals reflected the animal

RECEIVING THE MESSAGE

An animal that crosses your path, or is clearly in the wrong place (such as a bird in your home), might be significant and it is worth trying to connect with it[2]. Still your mind and notice the filament of the web of life that binds you and the animal. Focus on the emotions the animal invokes. What characteristics of the animal do you most identify with? By observing closely and being alert to the subtle energy exchange, try to ascertain the creature's message. Resist looking up the animal's symbolism, but focus on what *you* notice and what seems important to *you*. Its message is for you and you will not find it in books written by others.

spirits that Scythian shamans met in the otherworld[5]. Iroquois people of North America also revere animals that emerge from distant parts of the forest.

For people living on the Amur River in northeastern Siberia, a tiger met on a forest trail is a messenger from the spirits, and the shaman must establish its message. The tiger is *amba*, meaning "Master" (as with the bear, to use its real name would be disrespectful[6]). Farther along the Amur River, in northern China, Manchu people consider the tiger malignant, a bringer of unwelcome news. Clearly, the same animal has a different meaning in different communities. The same is true of the lion in Africa. In most of West Africa, the lion is king of the beasts and a symbol of power. People revere and celebrate the lion, believing that it was once a teacher of humans, that showed them how

▲ **A meeting with a bear** is seen as spiritually significant in many parts of the world; in Siberia people often call a bear "Older Brother".

to live with dignity[7]. Njajaan Njaay, the founder of the 13th-century Waalo kingdom in Senegal, spent his formative years in the wilderness among lions. In East Africa, however, people mock the lion for being lazy and being compared to a lion is an insult (although Nuer healers rely on its power, called "lion science")[8].

Whatever animal you meet, try to interpret its message. Connecting with animals at all levels — physically, emotionally and spiritually — opens up a world of possibilities. Give thanks for the spirit messengers, and recognize that no animal encounter is ever coincidental.

ANIMAL SPIRIT HELPERS

Light is fading in the rainforest as the Tupí shaman lies down upon the trail of fire ants. They swarm across his body, sinking their stings into his flesh and releasing their venom. Enduring the pain, he slips away from his physical body and enters the otherworld. Jaguar awaits and the shaman approaches this revered spirit with care. The animal is a source of great power for the shaman and his community.

JAGUAR

Tupí people faced annihilation at the hands of Portuguese settlers in the 16th century. Only a few groups now remain in the north Brazilian rainforest. Like initiates on a vision quest, Tupí shamans (*payé*) use the pain of ant stings to flood their body with sensation until their spirit breaks free and journeys to the otherworld[1]. It is an agonizing encounter with an animal helper in physical form. But the jaguar spirit is different. This spirit helper can only be reached in the otherworld. The *payé* described above probably wanted help for a hunt. He expected the animal he was calling on in spirit form to have all the usual characteristics of a jaguar, such as keen hunting skills, but also much more. Jaguar spirit has no limits to its power. It may be able to fly, swim underwater for long periods, and, most importantly, talk to the *payé*. Spirit animals reach back to a time when all animals were Animal People and could communicate with humans[2].

Jaguar spirit is not a spirit of a single jaguar but of all jaguars. Although Jaguar spirit works with many shamans, all shamans work with one Jaguar spirit. If you seek out Jaguar, it will be the same spirit, or at least a facet of it, that the Tupí *payé* met in the rainforest. We refer to the animal spirit as "Jaguar" instead of "a jaguar", as there is only one and that is its name.

PREDATORS AND PREY

The earliest evidence that people called upon animal spirits is in the painted caves of southern France and northern Spain, dating to the last Ice Age[3]. As well as thousands of images of prey species, a few predators appear, including big cats, bears and wolves. Small models of these predators were also carved, as touchstones of power for the hunters. The otherworldly nature of this art, coupled with patterns commonly seen in trance, suggests that these are shamanic visions, revealing the wisdom imparted by the spirits.

Sometimes, it is the prey rather than the predator species who help. Shamans (*puha*) of the North American Great Basin ask Antelope for its help in driving antelope prey toward hunters. These shamans, or "Antelope *Puha*", call upon no other animal spirit[4].

▶ **The lord of the rainforest**, the jaguar, is known as a supreme hunter and in its spirit form – as Jaguar – its help is sought by many South American tribespeople.

SEEKING HELP

If you need advice on an issue, an animal spirit may be able to help. If you want to meet a particular animal in the otherworld, then state its name as part of your intention; alternatively, just ask to meet the most appropriate animal spirit. As with any journey to the otherworld, call to your spirit guide to accompany you, and bear in mind that animal spirits can appear in both the upperworld and the lowerworld. In Borneo, most shamans agree that birds are located in the upperworld, overseen by a hornbill, whereas reptiles and fish occur in the lowerworld, overseen by a dragon. You may find a completely different arrangement on your travels and so, as with much of shamanism, you must trust what appears to you[5].

▲ **A sea spirit and her owl** feature in this 1979 print called *Talelayu Opiitlu*, by Canadian Inuit Kenojuak Ashevak.

You may want to gain a specific power from a spirit, such as the endurance of a wolf or the courage of a lion. If you do, ask the spirit animal if it will share some of its power with you. Whether transferred along the web of life, or presented in a box, make sure you hold onto this power when you return to this world. Ask your spirit guide how to achieve the transfer.

Asclepius, the Greek founder of medicine, relied upon the power of snakes; the annual shedding of skin was a symbol of the body healing itself. His patients dreamed of snakes, and these spirit animals revealed their cure[6]. The Maya of Central America also rely on

Snake, and spirit snakes appear to shamans (*h'men*) during initiation. They believe serpents hold the secret of regeneration, symbolizing death and rebirth[7].

TRAVELLERS AND TRICKSTERS

Some animals have characteristics that allow them to cross between habitats. Rainforest peoples revere jaguars not only for their hunting prowess but also for their ability to move between land, water and sky (the latter when they climb trees). In northern Eurasia, waterbirds similarly cross between earth, water and sky, and many Siberian people believe that spirits of waterbirds accompany dead souls to the afterlife, so that the night sky is streaked with their image – a smudge we call the Milky Way[8].

Occasionally, animal spirits may be indifferent or even hostile, but few are openly malignant. More common are animal spirits that play tricks, sometimes deliberately misleading us. These trickster spirits appear in many shamanic traditions[10]. In southwestern United States, Coyote is a spirit who hinders as much as he helps. In the far north-west, Raven is another trickster[11]. Working with these clownlike archetypes can be exasperating, but they teach through mockery and laughter, and show us not to hold onto anything too tightly. Our beliefs, standards and shamanic practice should be flexible enough to allow for a trickster. There is much wisdom in humour.

Whenever you have need, there is always an animal spirit to help. Sometimes the animal will make itself known to you, but at other times you will need to journey to the otherworld. As we shall see, some animals become such trusted helpers that individuals, families and even entire communities adopt them as symbols of identity. Animal spirits are the source of great power for shamans and their communities.

DREAMING OF ANIMALS

Yokut shamans from California work with Weasel, a creature associated with shamanic wisdom. Weasel approaches through dreams, indicating which other animals the shaman should call upon for help[9]. Animals also appear in the dreams of Zulu shamans (*sangoma*) from South Africa and are often the first sign that an individual is being called to initiate as a shaman.

If you dream of an animal, it might be a spirit trying to reach you. Upon waking, journey to the otherworld and meet the spirit again to find out what help it is offering. However, not all animals we encounter in dreams or the otherworld are helpers; some may serve an entirely different function. Mongolian shamans of the Asian steppes keep an unused hitching post outside their dwellings so that the spirits will have somewhere to tether their horses when they arrive[12]. The horses are also spirits but are of no relevance to the shaman – indeed, they wait outside.

53

ANIMAL TOTEMS

The Kyrgyz girl looks out over the pastures beneath the Celestial Mountains and reflects again on her family totem. Deer is a powerful creature and her grandmother, the shaman of the Bugu tribe, works with the spirit of the animal when she heals or tells people's fortunes. The girl is proud of her lineage because the tribe's first ancestor was a female deer, the Horned Mother. She can feel the animal's presence in her heart, radiating its power throughout her being.

TRIBAL TOTEMS

The Bugu tribe of Kyrgyzstan in central Asia believe that they descend from two young people raised by a female deer they call *müyüzdüü ene*, the Horned Mother. *Bugu* means "deer" in the Kyrgyz language. Other Kyrgyz tribes adopt different totems – such as the tribe known as Bagysh, meaning "elk" – but all retain echoes of the Horned Mother. Shamans (*bakshy* if male; *bübüs* if female) work with animal spirits, including these powerful totem spirits[1].

Zulu tribes from South Africa also adopt an animal as a totem. Strict taboos prevent the hunting or eating of the totem animal, which is generally an animal common to the area in which the tribe lives[2]. The totem animal is an extension of the tribe, and must be protected like any other member of the group.

In the Western world, families replace tribes, and there may be a totem animal associated with yours. If you have a name such as Fox, Bird or Fish then the identity of the animal is clear, but if not, you may need to journey to discover it. Your family may or may not have the characteristics of this animal, but it stands for who you are and where you originate, just as the deer does for the Kyrgyz girl.

In ancient northern Eurasia, an animal totem conferred a sacred dignity on its tribe. With qualities superior to those of humans, it represented the tribe's highest aspirations. Waterbirds are important across this region (see page 53), so it is not surprising that many tribes there have a bird as their totem. Farther east, the Buryat people adopt other animals, such as the blue bull of the Bulagat clan and the dogfish of the Ekhirit. However, unlike the Kyrgyz, Buryat shamans do not work with the spirits of totem animals[3].

Each lineage of the Yokut people of California has an inherited totem animal. The lineages venerate their animal and, like the Zulu, never hunt or eat it. If any hunter should catch another lineage's totem animal, the family will pay to redeem it. They celebrate their animal in seasonal dances: the rattlesnake ceremony in spring and the bear dance in autumn. Those with a coyote as their totem, clown about and generally disrupt events, as befits the trickster Coyote spirit[4].

▶ **Thunderbird power** is made present by this totem pole of the Kwakwaka'wakw people of Vancouver Island, Canada.

54

Certain positions within the Yokut tribe are associated with animal totems. An eagle represents the chief, for example, and an owl represents the shaman. Each animal protects the holder of the position as well as endowing him or her with its gifts. Is there a totem animal that represents what you do? If none is obvious, journey to the otherworld with an intention to find it. Ask the animal how you can incorporate its qualities into your role. Remember, however, that the totem animal serves the position first and foremost.

In Mexico and Guatemala, *tonal* spirits are animals personally associated with an individual[5]. As in the Chinese calendar, birth date determines the animal whose qualities will affect a person's life. Nähñu people of Mexico go further. They believe that whenever a child is born, an animal is simultaneously born in the mountains and the two are spiritually joined all their lives. This companion animal, or *rogi*, is a being in its own right[6]. If anything happens to a person's *rogi*, then the same will happen to the person (if the *rogi* should die, the person will die, too). Sorcerers send their *rogi* to assault those of their shaman enemies, and tribal shamans retaliate with their *rogi*. A shaman's *rogi* is generally an eagle or a puma, the region's most powerful daytime hunters, whereas a sorcerer's *rogi* is usually an owl or a fox, their nocturnal, darker equivalents.

If you had a *rogi*, what animal would it be? Whichever animals represent you, your family and your role in society, try to forge a closer bond with them and incorporate more of their strengths into your life[7]. There is now only one further animal spirit for you to meet and, even as you read these words, it is waiting for you. Can you already feel it in your heart, radiating its power throughout your being?

POWER ANIMALS

The adobe house is silent but for the chant of the Mazateco shaman as she calls to her spirit guide in the faint light of a candle. Her eyes are closed as her soul journeys inward. At once, her spirit guide is with her. She leans close to his furred face, sensing his hot breath, and whispers the contents of her heart. Puma listens before whispering back, "I am your *nagual*; I am always here for you. Take my power and be strong."

YOUR PROTECTOR

The word *nagual* (pronounced "na'wal") originates in the Aztec Nahuatl language, and has come to mean a spirit animal that is a person's principal protector. In Western shamanism we use the term "power animal". The Mazateco shaman above, from northern Oaxaca, Mexico, probably visits Puma often, relying on its strength and guidance, for herself and for her community[1]. In central Asia, Altai shamans call a power animal a *bayana*. Unusually, they believe that a *bayana* can be damaged by the trials of a individual's life, and they devote many shamanic sessions to its healing. This is a reminder of how closely connected some people are to their power animals[2].

A power animal is not a totem animal; it does not represent you or your lineage, and it is not a real animal, such as the *rogi* of the Nähñu people. You can only interact fully with your power animal in the otherworld. Everyone has a unique power animal, and it will have been with them throughout their entire life, whether the individual knows it or not[3]. *You* have a power animal. You might have met it in the otherworld and it may already be your spirit guide, or it may still be waiting for you to initiate contact. Journey now to find your power animal (see page 58) and begin one of the most important relationships you can have[4].

Do not be concerned about which animal comes to you — just trust that it is exactly right. It may be an animal that you remember being close to in childhood, or an animal that made its presence felt as you grew into an adult, or even an animal you barely recognize. It does not matter. Meet your animal now. The transfer of energy will fill you with vigour, but a power animal can do a lot more besides. All your questions, problems and issues are appropriate to take to your power animal. It will always have your best interests at heart.

Buryat shamans of Lake Baikal in southern Siberia received their power from the gods, or *tenger*. In an effort to end suffering on Earth, the sky god, Tengeri, sent an eagle to teach the people shamanism[5]. But they did not understand the language of the eagle and so it mated with a woman and gave her its power. She became the first shaman of the Buryat. In recent years Buryat shamans have increasingly worked with animal spirits. They now have personal animal protectors that bridge the divide between the totem animals we have already seen and power animals.

The Dagara, an agricultural people from the northwestern corner of Ghana, generally work only with animals they encounter in the local landscape. This restriction does not apply to Western shamanism, however, and your power animal can be of any type and from anywhere in the world[6]. There is no hierarchy among species of power animals — a mouse holds just as much power as an elephant. Most shamanic communities understand this implicitly, but many practitioners of Western shamanism keep their power animal secret and do not share its identity with people other than those they know and trust. Boasting of having a powerful animal as your personal guide seems egotistical and arrogant. Traditional shamans are much more open about their abilities. They make

▲ **Shamanic flags** beside a frozen Lake Baikal, Siberia. Here, a woman mated with an eagle to gain its divine power.

sure people know about their powerful spiritual allies, so that they will trust the shamans to cure their ailments. If you do share details of your guides, none of them will be offended and none will ever leave you. Your power animal exists solely to help, protect and guide you; why would it ever leave?

You may work with the power and energies of many animal spirits, but your power animal will always be at your side. Some people have more than one power animal and a few work with a large menagerie, but if you do it is likely that one will be particularly special and so close to you that it will sometimes be difficult to define the boundary between you. Some shamans even use their power animal as an avatar in the otherworld, and the word *nagual* also refers to a person who can take an animal's form. Buryat shamans sometimes battle in the form of their power animals, although if the animal should perish, the shaman will, too.

In Mexico, where shamans work with *naguals*, ancient sculpture from the Olmec civilization (the first to emerge in Central America) shows people who have transformed into jaguars. Archaeologists call these figures "were-jaguars", and similar creatures occur all over the world[7]. It may be that werewolves, which are prevalent in folklore around the Caucasus Mountains, also reflect shamans' ability to take the form of power animals. (For more on shapeshifting, see pages 68–71.)

Spend time getting to know your power animal. Learn its characteristics and its habits, and how it can help and empower you. Your power animal is part of you. Trust it implicitly, and you will have the confidence and ability to follow your shamanic path without fear or doubt. Your power animal is solely devoted to your welfare. It is always there for you – take its power and be strong.

◀ Jaguar spirit is represented here in a jade sculpture created in Mexico *c.* 900–800 BCE, during the Olmec era.

FIND YOUR POWER ANIMAL

Use this exercise to find your power animal, and accept that whatever animal appears is exactly right for you.

1. Start your "callback" drumming download (see page 6). Journey to the otherworld, setting your intention as: "I am journeying to find my power animal."

2. When you arrive, look around you. An animal might already be waiting for you — possibly one that you have met before on your travels — or you might have to move around and search.

3. Do not pursue an animal as soon as you see it, but continue travelling through the otherworld. Only after you have seen the same animal a number of times, or if an animal approaches you, should you ask if it is your power animal. If it replies that it is, you have found your power animal. If it replies that it is not, carry on looking.

4. When you find your power animal, spend time getting to know it, perhaps making repeat journeys for this purpose. When the drumbeat changes, follow its call to return.

5. Your power animal will now be waiting for you whenever you journey to the otherworld. If you cannot see it, just call and it will come to you.

DOMESTICATED ANIMALS

The bear is cub no longer. Once fed at the breast of a woman, it now eats the choicest delicacies that the Ainu community have to offer. Today, it is midwinter. The bear follows his handler willingly to the central altar. Hunters then surround him, holding bows and arrows. The first arrow thuds into his shaggy pelt and the bear cries in alarm. More follow until his breath gives out and he lies prostrate. The people give thanks for their animal and the power it has brought to them.

THE COMING OF SACRIFICE

After thousands of years hunting, killing and eating animals, humans found a new way to obtain their prey: they began to raise it themselves. Domestication has a long history, beginning around 13,000 years ago, when people first herded wild sheep and cattle[1]. It may be that when people in the Near East started to domesticate creatures such as the aurochs, the wild ancestor of cattle, it was for spiritual reasons rather than for food. Ice Age artists decorated cave walls with images of these huge beasts with their majestic horns, and it is likely that local hunters venerated them[2]. At many of the first settlements, such as Çatal Hüyük in Turkey, there are copious painted images and carvings of aurochs, often around shrines[3]. Perhaps the yearning of shamans to work with the spirit of these formidable creatures led to the capture of live ones. Real horns supplemented the images in the shrines.

Over time, captive aurochs are likely to have been bred, becoming more and more docile with each generation. Wild became tame, and spirit became sustenance.

Once people began to keep herds, they changed their attitude toward animals. These were no longer a quarry to be sought, but a commodity to own and raise. This changed the spiritual imperative of obtaining food, because it was no longer necessary to seek permission from the spirits in order to kill prey. Through ownership of animals, people could slaughter whatever they needed; humans were in charge now. However, they still owed a debt to their ancestors. The herd only existed because of the work and effort of those who had gone before. People needed to honour and pay back their ancestors in some way and they did this through offering some of their stock in sacrifice.

Hunters respect the animals they kill but they rarely offer them in sacrifice. During the Iron Age, with domestication established in Europe, sanctuaries were set aside in northern France for the ritual sacrifice of stock (c. 1st century BCE)[4]. In only one site is there any trace of a wild animal; all the others contain only the remains of domesticated stock. Animal sacrifice was to become a part of spirituality all over the world.

Consider your own attitude to animal sacrifice. Are blood rites abhorrent to you? This is another objection that traditional shamans would not understand. You may

see the act as *taking* the life of a creature; traditional people see it as *giving* the life of something they cherish. In domesticating animals, people moved from taking through the hunt to giving through sacrifice. Animals were often the most valuable commodity a person owned – they provided food, clothing, tools, fuel and, in the steppes of Asia, even the fabric of the house. Without their animals, people would die. Yet they still offered one or more of these life-giving creatures in gratitude. It was an act of incredible generosity.

In sacrificing the bear, the Ainu encompass the contradiction between wild and domestic (and between taking and giving)[5]. Now confined to Hokkaidō in Japan and Sakhalin in Russia, the Ainu raise a wild bear cub as an honoured member of the community, even suckling it at the breast of a woman. When the bear has grown up, people kill it in the ceremony described on page 59. The bear is *kamui*, or "god". In sacrificing the bear, people send the god back to heaven, and three days of festivity and many rituals honour the occasion.

The Igbo people from the rainforests of Nigeria believe that dogs can see spirits. This explains a strange part of the initiation ritual for a shaman (*dibïa*), which culminates in the sacrifice of a dog and the removal of its eyes[6]. The initiate receives these in place of his or, increasingly, her eyes, and is afterwards carried unconscious from the ceremonial hut with blood-encrusted leaves covering his or her face.

In Andean shamanism the domesticated guinea pig (*cuy*) takes a role in many healing ceremonies.

These creatures, raised as food for 7,000 years, give their lives in order that sick humans might heal.

▲ **Shepherd in Siberia**; in Neolithic times sheep and other domesticated animals were especially revered.

PETS AS POWER ANIMALS

Pets are at the centre of many people's lives, but despite being close to us, our animal companions rarely appear as power animals. This was not always so. For a short time following their domestication, animals such as cows and pigs were revered, the focus of many rituals[7]. People seemed to recognize the special ability domesticated animals possess in crossing worlds – in this case, from nature to culture. Cattle even seem to have been buried as substitute people in Neolithic tombs (c. 3,200 BCE)[8]. These animals later lost their prestigious status, although Indian communities still revere the cow. Nevertheless, if a domestic animal should appear to you in the otherworld, do not reject its advances. Working with living pets in the otherworld is difficult, but many people find that their companion animals appear after death.

Not all animals need a physical equivalent in this world to exist in the otherworld. As the next pages show, mythical animals abound. And your power animal will have characteristics that go way beyond anything its physical kin can accomplish. These are now yours to call upon. Why not visit and give thanks to your animal and the power it has brought you?

MYTHICAL CREATURES

· ·

The shaman drums an intoxicating beat. Her soul has long left the confines of the Altai steppe. In the lowerworld a huge, fishlike creature bars her path. Knowing that the creature can never be defeated in combat, the shaman uses her guile to gain safe passage. It is a dangerous path and the people pray fervently that she will be safe. Aware of the dangers, the shaman carries a fish amulet, knowing that it brings her power and safekeeping in her quest.

FANTASTICAL FOES AND FRIENDS

The shamans of the Altai steppe lands of eastern Siberia and Tuva have to pass the fish monster, or *ker-dyutpa*, every time they enter the otherworld[1]. The people in this region have known of this mythical creature for thousands of years. The Iron Age Pazyryk tribe, who once rode across these lands, buried their dead under huge mounds called *kurgans*. Incredibly, the beautifully tattooed skin of one chief has survived in the permafrost; covering his right leg is a giant fish, probably the same monster that shamans still encounter today[2]. It has even been identified by experts as a burbot, a species that can grow very large.

Tales of mythical creatures start by exaggerating the natural characteristics of animals. According to the Murut hill people of northern Borneo, the creator god, Aki Kaulung, punishes anyone who disrespects the forest[3]. This is policed by strange and terrifying creatures: the *angungkung* lion preys on the souls of those who laugh when entering the forest; the *tambailung* deer feeds on the bodies of transgressors. Both creatures are on their way to becoming mythical, especially as lions are not native to the region.

Many mythical animals can be allies. The Siberian "windhorse" rides like the wind across the steppes and carries shamans' messages to the heavens. Shamans use horse pelts to make their huge frame drums and, as they beat them to induce trance, they describe riding a horse to the otherworld. In the tomb of the Pazyryk chief above were two silver pendants and a whip handle in the shape of a horse[4]. The horse's head stretches forward, its front legs tucked under the jaw, its mane flying behind. Here might be the origin of the Siberian windhorse. The tomb also contained a saddle cover, embroidered with an image of a griffin[5]. Saddle covers in other burials are decorated with similar griffins, often attacking prey. The Pazyryk people raised stock, and so hunting was probably a leisure activity enjoyed by high-ranking individuals. Perhaps griffins were creatures hunters called upon to aid them, bringing the strength of the lion and the speed of the eagle. In Kazakhstan eagles are still used for hunting.

One mythical creature that exists all over the world is the dragon. In China dragons were a symbol of imperial authority and have adorned precious objects for over 8,000 years, with Xinglongwa people from

Inner Mongolia the first to depict them[6]. Working with these auspicious creatures brings great power. In Europe some Iron Age people decorated their swords with images of sinuous dragons, with eyes picked out in red stones[7]. The owner of such a weapon may have called on the power of the dragon before entering battle, and his or her unfortunate opponent may have been hypnotized by the red glare of the dragon's eye.

If you ever have need of special powers, ask your power animal to introduce you to a mythical animal. It could be any one of myriad fantastic beasts[8]. As with anything that crosses boundaries, hybrid animals (half-human and half-animal) seem especially attuned to shamanism. Chiron, for example, the half-human, half-horse centaur of Greek myth, passed on his prowess to the great heroes Heracles and Jason, and also disclosed the secrets of healing to Asclepius.

In medieval times (and in some areas of the world today), animal parts were collected for their curative properties or (as in ancient shamanic practice) used as good-fortune charms. You might like to carry a symbol of an animal spirit. Your charm can be purely symbolic but it can still connect you to the creature's energy and strength. As the next pages show, such an amulet can bring you power and safekeeping in your quest.

▶ **Three-clawed dragons** adorn these 16th-century tiles from Shanxi, China. The dragon was a key imperial symbol.

FUR AND FEATHER

In a cloud of thick incense, the Tsugaru shaman chants with her clear, lilting voice to bring down the spirits. It is a dangerous time and she fingers her rosary of different animal parts constantly, finding the right animal power to keep her client safe. Each animal part offers a repository of spiritual power for whenever she has need.

OBJECTS OF POWER

Like the Ainu (see page 60), Tsugaru people live in northern Japan, but their shamanic tradition has more in common with that of Siberia. Their name means, in the Ainu language, "those who live at the base of the sun". *Itako* are blind Tsugaru shamans, usually women, who channel messages from deities, divine answers to questions and heal the sick. The animal parts in their rosaries are mostly given to them by local Matagi hunters[1]. A variety of teeth, claws, horns and bones allow the shaman to protect those whom she is healing, to drive out malevolent entities and to keep her own body pure and safe from harm.

Yaka shamans (*ngaanga ngoombu*) of the woods and savannah of the southwest of the Democratic Republic of Congo also rely on animal parts for divination[2]. These allow the shaman to connect to the web of life and to access information from spirits. Any part may be used, including bones, fur, teeth, nails or hooves, as each is capable of channelling the entire animal. The parts are kept at a shrine, usually in a basket. Any ambiguous or transformational creatures, such as those that cross between habitats, are favoured, reflecting the shamanic focus on transcending boundaries. Other favoured animals include those with exceptional abilities, such as being able to see in the dark or having the stamina to run all day.

You may baulk at gathering actual animal parts, but some cause few moral problems. Collecting feathers that a bird has dropped is easy (but check before gathering feathers from protected species, even if they have fallen naturally, as laws vary). The Huichol of Mexico collect feathers from birds they admire for their hunting abilities, such as hawks, and carry them in baskets to Wirikuta (see page 14)[3]. Huichol *mara'akame* make feathered wands from the colourful plumage of parrots, using them for healing and communicating with the gods while in trance. If you find a feather, try journeying to the spirit of the bird while holding it in your hand. This might also reveal which species of bird it came from.

Nepalese shamans wear headdresses of peacock or mountain pheasants, the rainbow plumes providing a bridge for the spirits. In Brazil, Aparai *payé* wear headdresses made from the feathers of jungle birds to re-enact the creation story in which the Great Spirit wore the flashing plumage of a bird. This demonstrates a connection to spiritual power and the avian guide spirits[4]. In the mountainous far west of China, *duangong* are shamans of the Qiang people, an indigenous group who can trace their origins back to prehistory. All the tools the *duangong* use in their rituals are sacred but they worship only one: a monkey skull. The shaman keeps it in a shrine wrapped in layers of brown and white paper and every year adds a further wrapping[5]. The monkey skull represents the first *duangong*, another example of shamanic wisdom crossing from the animal to the human realm.

You could give your animal parts a permanent home where you can go to absorb some of their power. In the Altai Mountains of Tuva, shamans enshrine the paw of a bear and bring it out and place it on their altar when undertaking shamanic work. You may want to do something similar. Alternatively, you could keep your animal symbols with you, either on a string or rosary like the Tsugaru *itako*, or perhaps in a small pouch. If you become tired during the day, touching them will give you an immediate injection of energy and power.

Among the Cape Nguni, a group of Xhosa and Zulu people in South Africa, *sangomas* keep animal parts in a goatskin bag and use them in healing. Especially efficacious are otter and mongoose skins and swatches of hippo hide[6]. Male *sangomas* also wear a headdress of white feathers, a colour symbolic of clarity.

Inuit people of Greenland retain the bones of animals for personal protection, calling upon the spirit of the animal for its aid. Since a hunter always treats the quarry with respect, the animal is usually willing to oblige. The bone becomes a repository of the animal's spirit and a container for its power.

Killing an animal for spiritual reasons is not acceptable in the West and if you work with Tiger, Elephant or Puma, you are unlikely to find a tooth or claw from an animal that has died naturally. However you can buy a picture or model of your animal, or create your own. Wear marks on small Ice Age sculptures of animals show these were handled regularly, as people called on their power[7]. Recordings of roars, calls and other animal sounds are also available online.

Zuni people of the southeastern United States carve small stone models or fetishes of animals that capture the creatures' power. A hunter carries fetishes of predatory animals to bring success, and will offer the helping fetish blood from the slain beast[8]. The neighbouring Navajo use fetishes of horses, cattle and sheep to protect herds from disease and to aid fertility.

Ask your power animal or other animal spirit to fill your amulet or fetish with its power, so that it becomes a sacred object. Always combine your use of these items with journeying to the actual spirit of the animal, and also find out whether your fetish needs any special treatment. Each of the animal spirits that you meet can provide a repository of spiritual power for whenever you have need.

65

ANIMAL RULERS

Game has become scarce and the Inuit shaman has journeyed to the bottom of the ocean in search of Inua, Mother of the Sea. He enters her lair cautiously, his power animal beside him. Suddenly Inua springs and the shaman tumbles backward. He claws himself upright and battles the furious, filth-covered spirit. When he has prevailed, he begins to cleanse Inua of the build-up of filth caused by all the community's taboo transgressions, identifying each and every lapse. Finally, he combs her matted hair. Now she is beautiful again, Inua will release the game animals and the community will have food. The *angakkuq* returns, upbraiding those who broke taboo, the power of the otherworld channelled into him[1].

FEMALE AND MALE RULERS

Like the Greenland Inuit, the ancient Greeks saw the ruler of the animals as female rather than male. In the *Iliad*, the great epic of the Trojan War, Homer speaks of Potnia Theron, the "Mistress of the Animals"[2]. Homer was probably referring to Artemis, the Greek goddess of hunting, who both protected and preyed upon her charges. Potnia Theron was already ancient in Homer's time. During the Minoan civilization and in early Mycenaean times, the Mistress appears on jewellery and other artwork as an upright woman grasping an animal, demonstrating her dominance over nature. She reappears just before the Classical period of Greek history (beginning *c.* 5th century BCE), before Artemis assumes her identity[3].

Across parts of Siberia there is a Master of the Animals, and the (usually male) shaman may have to marry the Master's sister or daughter in an elaborate ritual[4]. When the shaman becomes a son-in-law, the Master will release a dowry of game animals, and the shaman's spirit brothers-in-law will help in the hunt. The belief in a Master of the Animals is common among hunting people and relates to the ambiguity of the hunt[5]. Asking for (and receiving) permission before hunters take life changes the act from wanton killing to fair exchange. Instead of a spiritually polluting act, killing for food is part of the bargain struck with nature, personified as the Master of the Animals. It is a means of ensuring sustainability, both spiritually with the exchange of human for animal souls (see page 47), but also physically, with overhunting having dire consequences if the Master withholds further game. We desperately need a similar approach in the West.

The Celts also recognized a Master of the Animals, depicting him on the late Iron Age Gundestrup cauldron from Denmark as an antlered chief flanked by animals of the forest[6]. Later images of this figure appear, sometimes with cloven hooves, as Cernunnos, the Celtic god of abundance and the otherworld.

In Amazonia, *payé* negotiate not only with the Master of the Animals but also with the Master of

the Fish[7]. *Payé* transform themselves into bubbles of air so that they can stay underwater and ask the Master to release more fish into the rivers. The Master of the Animals can send illness, snakes or bad weather to punish those who kill animals without permission. It can be hard to appease him, as he hides in the tangled vegetation of the hills. He usually appears in the form of a red dwarf, dressed as a hunter and carrying a bow.

The Master or Mistress of the Animals has many forms, but the actual image is immaterial. If you journey to meet him or her, just trust the spirit that appears, which may not be similar to these examples. You probably make use of animals as food and clothing or by taking medicine that has been tested on them. If you have never asked permission for this, do so now, and be prepared for the possibility that the Master or Mistress might want something in return. You may also want to follow tribal shamans in asking how to

▲ **Master of the Animals**, shown on the Danish Gundestrup cauldron (2nd or 1st century BCE), his chiefdom signalled by a torc. The tree may symbolize a portal to the otherworld.

reduce your burden on the Earth by consuming less and ensuring that natural resources regenerate. This approach has much relevance to us today.

If you find you must marry a spirit as part of your journey to the Master or Mistress, you could act out your role just as Siberian shamans do. Wearing the skin, antlers and other identifying characteristics of the animal, the shaman moves, sounds and behaves just like the animal itself. In a way, the shaman becomes the animal, and, as we shall see next, this is an effective means of embodying the power of another creature. The ancient practice of shapeshifting allows the power of the otherworld to be channelled into you.

SHAPESHIFTING

The shaman has trained five years for this moment, ever since he left his Huichol village and devoted his life to wolf shamanism. He has already sung and danced with the pack that frequents these hills and now, under a full moon, he will become one of them. Performing five complete somersaults, one for each night that he will remain a wolf, the shaman's form begins to change. Nose elongates to snout, hands become paws and a tail grows bushy. The shaman howls his delight and lopes to the waiting pack. It is one of the most powerful acts a shaman can ever perform.

SOUL–SHIFTING

The Huichol practice of shapeshifting into a wolf stems from the myth that in the beginning humans were wolves[1] After they gained great knowledge through eating the peyote cactus, Great Spirit gave the wolves a choice: to live as animals or as humans. They chose the latter, but their Huichol descendants can still learn to take the form and attributes of the wolf. The power a shaman gains through this process is substantial.

In Amazonia, *payé* shapeshift into the form of a jaguar. Significantly, this is the only animal outside the control of the Master of the Animals and this gives the *payé* considerable freedom when they take on the animal's characteristics[2]. When *payé* shapeshift, their internal organs move around so that the heart is on the back, reflecting the widespread belief that the otherworld of the spirits is the opposite of this world. Among the Desana and Tukano communities of the Columbian rainforest, people believe that dead *payé* transform into jaguars. The Kogi Indians of the uplands of Columbia call themselves "children of the jaguar", believing, like the Huichol, that they descend from an animal[3]. Shamans ingest a plant they call *nebbi kuái*, or "jaguar's testicles", which gives them the sensation they are shapeshifting into feline form. Once shamans have become jaguars, they can heal illness, interpret omens and dreams, and protect their community with supernatural power.

Huichol *mara'akame* who transform into wolves comment that they still see their human form when they observe themselves, as it is the soul that shifts and not the body. While there are stories of were-jaguars and were-wolves, this sort of physical change is not the aim of shamanic shapeshifting. To understand this, try the exercise on page 71[4]. You will feel your power animal inside you merging its thoughts, characteristics and power with your identity. This is not possession – your power animal does not take control of your body – but embodiment, in which your consciousness shifts to include the awareness of another being.

▶ **Elaborate animal masks**, such as this one of a lion king, are often used in the rituals and dance of Bali and Java.

68

70

When shapeshifting, remember that the hierarchy of animals in this world is unimportant; all animals are equally powerful in the otherworld. In Papua New Guinea male shamans transform into birds while female shamans transform into frogs – both seen as extraordinarily powerful in the otherworld.

In the rainforests of Malaysia, Batek shamans (*putao*) shapeshift differently so that their awareness is projected into an animal, rather than their soul remaining in their body. Shaman-tigers protect their communities, especially from real tigers that might otherwise attack (up to 800 of these magnificent creatures still patrol the forest home of the Batek)[5]. In eastern Java, were-tigers protect villages, and at the climax of the traditional *barong* dance, in which different animal spirits appear on stage, a masked man embodies the spirit of the were-tiger.

Siberian shamans also use masks, headdresses and costumes when they shapeshift, wearing the pelt of a reindeer or a bear and the feathers of a bird. Like the Amazonian *payé*, the costumes reflect the reversal of the spirit world and often the skeleton of the creature is depicted on the outside. Wearing the costume helps

▲ **Ritual mask** created by the Yup'ik people of southwestern Alaska and used during transformative dance ceremonies to make the otherworld visible.

the shaman to assume rapidly the awareness and characteristics of the animal. Again, it is the soul that shifts and not the body.

Evenki shamans of southern Siberia effect the change not through donning a costume but by spending a considerable period alone in the forest, reproducing the whisper of the spirits[6]. Eventually, awareness shifts and an animal spirit enters the shaman's body. Imitating the animal, the shaman returns to the community brimming with newfound power.

You might want to obtain or make a costume that reflects your power animal and helps you to shapeshift easily into its form. Instead of a real pelt, you could use fake fur or just a symbol of the creature. Many Siberian shamans hang small metal shapes that depict their spirit helpers from their drum or costume. If you work with a bird, you could make a headdress out of feathers or even wear a cloak entirely covered in them. Or you can limit your attire to just a mask if a complete costume is too ambitious. The people who colonized northern Europe after the last Ice Age fashioned the heads and antlers of red deer into masks that they used in hunting ceremonies[7]. They may have also worn pelts of deer, but only the masks have survived.

Among indigenous people of Alaska, shamans (*tungralik*) use masks (*kinaroq*) in healing rituals[8].

Wearing the mask allows the *tungralik* to draw upon the transformative strength of the creature depicted and embody its power. Some masks can be so large that *tungralik* need the help of others to support them. Among the Iroquois of northeastern North America, the False Face Society is devoted to mask-healing, their wooden masks embodying the power of healing and transferring it to the healer when worn[9]. Both Alaskan and Iroquoian people treat masks as living creatures and care for them accordingly. For people in Bali, wooden masks called *tapel* are so sacred that only consecrated carvers can shape them from the tenget tree[10]. They contain and embody the spirit of the animal, which is usually mythological, and they lie covered with fabric in temples when not in use. They are not art but sacred objects, and would never be put on display. If you create a mask depicting your power animal, treat it with the same reverence. It embodies the connection with your power animal and can bring your animal's form and power into this world. In effect, the mask becomes a portal between realities.

Shapeshifting incorporates all that you have learned so far about animal shamanism, including your relationship with wild creatures, your interaction with animals' physical and spiritual forms, your encounters with the Master or Mistress of the Animals, your use of power animal symbols and, finally, your ability to change into your power animal's form. Shapeshifting is one of the most powerful acts you can ever perform.

BECOME YOUR POWER ANIMAL

This exercise will show you how to shapeshift into your power animal, and it can also be used to shapeshift into other animals as you gain confidence with the technique.

1. Start your continuous drumming track (see page 6). Journey to the otherworld, setting your intention as: "I am journeying to shapeshift into my power animal."

2. Find your power animal and ask permission to shapeshift into its form.

3. If the answer is yes, immediately return from the otherworld, letting the drumming beat continue.

4. Stand in a relaxed posture (opening your eyes if you wish) and feel your power animal within you. Let the awareness of your own body fall away. Feel your animal breathe, then stretch its limbs. Finally, begin to move.

5. You are now shapeshifting. Do you feel the power of your animal coursing through you? This is now yours to access. Move and feel the power within you.

6. When you want to stop, become aware of your own body and let the awareness of your animal fall away until you are back in your human form. Send thanks to your power animal, who is returning to the otherworld.

PLANT

SACRED PLANTS

The shaman knows that the soul of the fisherman rests with the water people. Swallowing a mix of ayahuasca and other plants, he waits until the bitter brew fills his body with power. Singing songs of the spirits, he calls upon his guides to take him to the riverbed. There he wrestles the fisherman from the grip of a mermaid, relying upon the power of the ayahuasca to bring him safely back. The spirit of the plant is the shaman's most important guide and teacher.

74

ENTHEOGENS

Ayahuasca is one of many alkaloid-containing plants consumed by shamans worldwide to induce trance. The alkaloids enter the blood stream and travel to the brain where they affect the nervous system, often causing a shift in consciousness that may result in visions[1]. These can often be profound and bring individuals into direct contact with the spirit world. Many shamanic people call these plants "entheogens", a Greek word that loosely means "that which reveals God". It places emphasis on the sacred nature of these plants, in contrast to the medical term, hallucinogen.

◀◀ **The Ecuadorian rainforest** offers a huge variety of plants to local herbalists and healers.
▶ **A green peyote cactus** is central to this yarn painting by shaman José Benítez Sánchez. Other peyote are shown crowned as sacred with antlers.

Indeed, Inca people refer to the coca plant as the "divine leaf", and consume it in spiritual ceremonies[2].

USING AYAHUASCA

Throughout the Amazon rainforest, *payé*, or more specifically *ayahuasqueros*, use a brew made from ayahuasca to access the spirit world and obtain wisdom and healing powers[3]. Training is long and arduous, requiring sequestration in the forest and strict diets abstaining from salt, sugar, alcohol and sometimes fat. Repeated ingestion of ayahuasca enables the apprentice to befriend the plant and learn its secrets[4]. Eventually, the spirits will teach the *ayahuasquero* songs, or *icaros* – invocations of the spirit. Singing the words of an *icaro* transfers spiritual power through the *ayahuasquero* and into the world[5].

The Shuar of the rainforests of Ecuador and Peru believe that ayahuasca reveals the true reality. Even infants are given a diluted brew to help them to see the real world and to connect with an ancestor spirit that will help them through their first few years[6].

Ayahuasca by itself has little effect on the human body; *ayahuasqueros* mix it into a brew utilizing up to 30 plant additives. With 40,000 plants in the forest, it seems incredible that anyone would have discovered the right mix through trial and error. The *ayahuasqueros* would say that the plant itself taught them all they needed to know and so they call ayahuasca, along with several other species, "teacher plants". By causing trance, ayahuasca reveals and allows access to the world of the spirits, as we saw in the case of the Amazonian *ayahuasquero* who journeyed to the riverbed to rescue the soul of a fisherman[7].

OTHER ENTHEOGENS

At the heart of the Bwiti religion of Gabon and Congo is the entheogen *iboga*, which people prepare by pulverizing the root to a paste or else infusing it in water[8]. Its effects, described as "breaking open the head", allow entry to the spirit world. As in many African traditions, ancestors are paramount, and *iboga* enables people to contact and speak to them directly.

Some shamans breathe in entheogens as snuff. *Epená* is a snuff widely used by *payé* in western Amazonia, made from the inner bark of the Virola tree species[9]. *Payé* cannot speak directly with the spirits after taking *epená*, but have to communicate through a go-between, the "snuff person", who lives at the heart of the Milky Way. Taíno people, the indigenous inhabitants of the Caribbean, also inhaled snuff, called *cohoba*, to facilitate their shamanic journeys[10]. It may have been made from the yopo tree, but as colonization wiped out the Taíno within 60 years of Columbus landing, what we know about their rituals is pieced together from archaeological remains and scant historical sources. It seems that the *cohoba* ritual took place in a cave, the shaman sitting on a special curved stool. The shaman used a long spatula to induce vomiting, then the snuff was administered with a Y-shaped pipe, causing the shaman's eyes to bulge and run with dark liquid as the soul soared up to the world of the spirits. Nähñu shamans of Mexico inhale the smoke of *santa rosa* (a cannabis extract) in order to see inside their patients and read the story of their lives.

SACRED PLANTS WITHIN THE COMMUNITY

Ingestion of an entheogen can sometimes be part of a ceremony, with prayers and ritual to prepare those who are going to consume it. In the Native American Church, large congregations come together to revere peyote, a small desert button cactus, as a teacher and as divine medicine. Some view taking it as equivalent to the sacrament of Christianity, but ceremonies are a syncretism of various religious traditions. During San Pedro ceremonies (named after the San Pedro cactus native to the mountains of Peru), a shaman purifies participants using tools from the *mesa* (see page 36), often blowing perfumed water over their bodies[11]. People usually consume the San Pedro cactus as a brew, as with ayahuasca. Its effects are gentler, however, and do not always include visions, but most who drink it say that it gives them an incredible feeling of connection to the world around them.

The importance of an entheogen to a community is often reflected in the existence of myths about the plant. Datura is an entheogen used by the Zuni people of the southwestern United States, who chew the root to activate its effects. According to the Zuni, the plant originates from a brother and sister called Aneglakya and A'neglakyatsi'tsa, who live deep within the Earth but once visited the surface to gather wisdom[12]. People recognized them by the flowers they wore in their hair. When the siblings returned to their realm, the flowers remained and became datura, known for its large, bell-shaped flowers. Datura, still called Aneglakya, contains all that the siblings learned about the world.

In the Western world most entheogens are illegal, and in Europe there is very little tradition regarding their use. Rock art from the Scandinavian Bronze Age depicts *Amanita muscaria*, or fly agaric (which is known by its distinctive red and white cap) in the context of dancing and drumming figures[13]. These may have been shamanic ceremonies, and the Sámi people, indigenous to Scandinavia, once used this mushroom in their rituals. Other plants may have been used in prehistory to effect trance, but none retains a tradition to match those in the Americas.

Trying entheogens is a personal decision. Those in the Western world who do so often overlook that traditional people approach these plants only after long and arduous training, through which they prove themselves ready to meet such an exalted teacher. Shamans also use entheogens as regular medicine to cure a wide array of conditions without the patient necessarily experiencing trance. Moreover, as the next pages show, there are many different ways of working with sacred plants that are not entheogens. Indeed, one such plant may even prove to be one of your most important guides and teachers.

SPIRITS IN THE GREEN

Hunched in his hut, the Kamsá *payé* sings songs to carry him to the realm of the spirits, a mirror of his forest homeland. Once there, he approaches the spirit of a plant he wishes to know better, singing songs of greeting. The plant spirit turns to flee, but stops upon hearing the song. Over time the *payé* will befriend the spirit and obtain its help and guidance.

ROUTES TO THE SPIRITS

When the Kamsá and Inga *payé* of the Sibundoy valley of the Columbian rainforest want to learn about a particular plant, they approach its spirit and ask[1]. This is how many Amazonian *payé* learn traditional forms of medicine. They use entheogens to induce trance and meet the plant spirits, but you can achieve the same by journeying while listening to drumbeat.

In the Amazon, forging a relationship with a plant spirit can take years and require abstention from all sorts of usual foods, as well as celibacy and long periods in the forest. During that time, an initiate will regularly consume the plant in ceremonies and rituals. If you are drawn to any plant, ask its spirit to reveal a diet to follow while you work with it. There may be certain types of food, activities or even thoughts you should avoid. If the plant is agreeable, and you are certain it is not poisonous, put a small piece of it on your tongue when you journey to meet its spirit, so that you absorb some of its essence into your body.

In Amazonia, initiates train under a specialist plant shaman (*vegetalista*), who teaches the practical and medicinal applications of the plant as well as its spiritual traditions. Try researching your plant's practical uses, looking at old folklore and traditions as well as modern research. Old herbals can often reveal much about a plant's spiritual energy and are a treasure trove of wisdom to the modern shaman. You can also follow the Krahó *payé* of Brazil and ask your power animal or other animal spirits about plants.

◀ **Peyote collection** by a shaman of the Huichol people of central Mexico, to whom this plant is sacred.

78

Amazonian people often relate that animals teach them about plants.

Once you have journeyed to a plant and followed any diet it gives you, it may become a permanent ally like your power animal. The shamans of the Altai Mountains of Tuva believe that a person's *nagual* comprises an animal and a plant spirit[2]. Both are equally powerful. Carlos Castaneda was once asked by his teacher Don Juan to grow jimsonweed, a type of datura. Castaneda had to follow set rituals at every stage of cultivation if the plant was to accept him[3].

Although Castaneda insisted that Don Juan was a Yaqui shaman, from around Mexico's Sonora desert, it is the Huichol further south in Mexico who specialize in plant use. They have three sacred plants: the peyote cactus, tobacco (a type with nicotine levels sufficient to cause trance) and *kiéri*, a type of datura. The Huichol both revere and fear *kiéri*, and anyone wanting to work with it has to follow a five-year apprenticeship, regularly consuming small doses of the plant[4]. In large quantities, *kiéri* causes terrifying visions and can even lead to madness and death. It is the plant preferred by sorcerers, who use its power to curse.

All plant spirits (like animal spirits) are equally powerful in the otherworld. While trees capture the hearts of many, do not overlook the plants at their base. You can befriend the spirit of even the most inconspicuous weed, and obtain its help and guidance.

MEETING A PLANT SPIRIT

Plants make incredible teachers, although this tuition may be lengthy and involved[5]. Aboriginals describe some Dreamtime beings as resembling plants, but few origin stories teach that people descend from plants (see box, page 81). Yet all animal life diverged from a plant ancestor some two million years ago — plants really are our relations. Treat plant spirits with respect, even reverence, and focus on the connection between you.

1. If you are meeting the spirit of a plant that grows locally, put a small piece of it in your hands or on your tongue (ask for the plant's permission before cutting what you need). Start your "callback" drumming download (see page 6). Journey to the otherworld, setting your intention as: "I am journeying to meet the spirit of [name of plant]."

2. Look out for anything that catches your eye in the otherworld (remember that the spirit may not resemble its plant). If it appears several times, ask its identity. Your power animal and other spirit guides will help.

3. When you meet the spirit of the plant, get to know it in the same way you have befriended other spirits.

4. Return to the tunnel when the drumbeat changes and come back to this world.

MEETING THE TREES

The Oroqen hunters assemble around a birch tree at the edge of their settlement. The youngest among them, their best woodworker, carves the face of the mountain god into the tree's trunk. The design stands out dark against the white bark. The hunters bow their heads and whisper homage to the god and to their ancestor spirits. The tree is a portal to the otherworld and through its form the spirits can hear.

CONNECTING WITH TREES AND THEIR SPIRITS

During the Cultural Revolution in the middle of the last century, the Oroqen people of northern China were forced by the Communists to abandon their shamanic beliefs. They held a grand ritual over several days to send the spirits away for ever. The last shaman (named Chuonnasuan after the bird noise he made as a child) died in October 2000. But the spirits did not leave entirely, and traditional Oroqen hunters still carve the face of the mountain god into birch trees[1].

Trees seem to embody characteristics that we all can

◀ **False Face Society mask**, used by the Iroquois in healing ceremonies as a living embodiment of a spirit.

recognize as special, even sacred. It is revealing to watch people relaxing in a park — most will choose to sit under or close to a tree. When the Iroquois of northeastern North America make masks for the False Face Society, they carefully craft them from wood to contain and honour a particular spirit from the forest[2]. Originally, the masks were carved from a living tree, and only on completion was the physical link severed.

Ashanti *akomfo* from Ghana spend the last night of their initiation alone in the blackness of the forest, surrounded by trees. From here the spirits, including their guardian spirit, will emerge (see page 21).

In Madagascar, when an elderly Zafimaniry couple die, their descendants continue to add carvings to their wooden house, which stands as a cenotaph to their memory[3]. The wood represents the couple and establishes their eternal permanence in this world.

Aboriginals of Australia believe that a helping spirit resides in a *minggah* tree, and that harming one will harm the other (see page 35). The ancient Greeks also thought that each tree contains a *hamadryade*, or spirit. Killing the tree meant killing the *hamadryade*, so the gods punished mortals who harmed trees.

The ancient Greeks believed that there were also spirits to represent all trees of the same species. Dryads represent oak trees, while the Meliae belong to ash trees; the Epimeliads to apple trees, and the Caryatids to walnut trees[4].

TREES AS PORTALS

Forests have long been considered sacred. The ancient Druids of Britain and Gaul met in woodland clearings they called *nemeton*, meaning groves. The Roman poet Lucan described such a grove as a place where no animal would venture, and where gales and lightening had no effect[5]. Strange sounds emerged from the ground and oaks burst into flames without causing harm. Such magical places inverted phenomena from this world and may have been portals to the otherworld, as the otherworld is often seen as an inversion of this one. Try journeying to the otherworld via a tree, entering a hole in its trunk and then travelling up to the upperworld or down to lowerworld. Then do the same with an inverted tree (see box, below). Have the worlds now switched places? Experiment to discover which route you prefer.

Journey to meet the *hamadryade* of your favourite tree, following the process you used to gain a plant as an ally (see page 79). A tree spirit can be an incredible source of shamanic power. You might harvest, in a sacred manner (see pages 84–5), a piece of your tree's wood or some fruit, nuts or berries. Spend time with the spirit and visit your tree's physical form. Speak to it kindly. The tree you have chosen is a portal to the otherworld and through its form the spirits can hear.

THE WORLD TREE

In shamanism, trees often provide an *axis mundi* joining all three worlds of the shaman[6]. The mighty ash Yggdrasil of Norse mythology stretches from the heavens to the underworld, and Odin hung upon it for nine days to obtain shamanic knowledge. In Siberia, Buryat shamans call their World Tree, a birch, Udesi Burkhan, or "guardian of the door". The World Tree of the Zulu of South Africa is Sima-Kade, or "one who stands for all time". All people are said to descend from the union of Sima-Kade and a goddess of human form — one of the few instances where a first ancestor is from the plant kingdom. The Maya of Central America call their World Tree, a type of ceiba, Wacah Chan. The *h'men* use it to access all three realms of the otherworld.

The Sámi of Lapland offered sacrifices at altars that they made by thrusting trees top first into the earth[7]. By inverting a tree the Sámi gave it the properties of, and so formed a portal to, the otherworld. Like the Druids, they brought the essence of the otherworld into this world. Evidence of similar practices in the Bronze Age has been found on England's east coast. At Seahenge, an inverted tree had a flat platform within its roots that may have been used for offerings, while another close by probably held a coffin.

There seems to be a strong connection between people and trees, as if we recognize them as entities that, like us, have a consciousness of their own. For the ancient Greeks, it was the Dryads who were the consciousness of oak trees; other tree species had their own presiding spirits.

GATHERING THE HARVEST

Druids cloaked in white assemble under the sacred oak at night. A pair of oxen glint in the light of a flickering brand. A cry of acclamation, and a white cloak is unfolded. One of the Druids ascends the oak, carrying a sickle in the shape of the new moon. He offers prayers to the gods, then cuts a bunch of mistletoe that falls onto the cloak. The Druids have gathered their harvest of both plant and spirit.

HARVESTING RITUALS

In his 37-volume *Natural History*, the Roman historian Pliny the Elder described the Druids' elaborate ritual for gathering mistletoe, their most sacred plant[1]. They seem to have treated other plants with similar, almost bizarre, respect. Druids may only gather *selagos*, a type of figwort, if they wear white clothes back to front, are barefoot, and have left offerings of bread and wine. They can only gather *samolus*, a type of brookweed, with their left hand after fasting. Vervain is even more complicated. Anyone wishing to harvest this herb must first offer honeycombs, then draw a circle around the plant using an iron blade, grasp the plant in the left hand and hold it aloft. This can only be done when Sirius, the Dog Star, shines, but not the sun or moon. After picking, sunlight must not fall on the herb[2].

Perhaps these strange procedures were done to blur the boundaries between this world and the other. If the otherworld is a reversal of this world, it makes sense for the Druids to wear clothes back to front, use their left hands, go barefoot and refrain from eating. Even the astrological requirements are times betwixt-and-between. By piercing the veil between the worlds, a Druid can access the realm of the spirits, collecting not only the physical plant but also its spirit.

Always pause and ask permission before taking a leaf from a plant. If you want something more substantial or if you need it for shamanic work, you should first journey to the spirit of the plant, asking permission to gather it and seeking the spirit's advice on how to harvest, store or use the plant.

When Huichol pilgrims reach Wirikuta, home of their ancestors, they gather the sacred peyote cactus. Peyote formed when their god Kauyumári, meaning "Elder Brother Deer", walked the Earth singing sacred songs. He travelled along threads of the web of life, which converged at Wirikuta, where the god's footprints formed peyote cactus. Gathering peyote is not a harvest but a hunt for Kauyumári. Pilgrims stuff their mouths with tobacco, another plant sacred to the Huichol, and set out with bows and arrows. When they spot a cactus, they shoot it with an arrow before severing it at the root, never harvesting too much[3].

GROWING PLANTS

A good way of forming a relationship with a plant you wish to harvest is to grow it yourself. To counter

▲ *The Druids Bringing in the Mistletoe* by George Henry (1890) was inspired by archaeological excavations in Scotland and Pliny's description of the mistletoe ceremony.

the loss of rainforest plants used by Mayan healers in Belize, the Ix Chel Foundation set up a reserve to grow medicinal plants[4]. When an area of rainforest is under threat, the Foundation gathers shoots and seeds for the reserve. Plants are harvested in a traditional manner, and used in the local community and beyond. When Castaneda worked with jimsonweed (see page 79),

Don Juan asked him to plant a cutting and to tend it while it grew. Don Juan knew that, to form an intimate bond with a plant, you have to know it as a friend.

Journey to the spirit of the plant and ask if there is a special ritual you should perform when planting seeds[5]. For example, modern Druids plant seeds as part of their spring equinox ceremony. You may want to find out about biodynamic gardening, which harnesses the power of the sun, moon and stars[6]. This approach has ancient roots – Druids considered astronomical configurations when harvesting their crops. It also acknowledges that the plant is integrated in the web of life that stretches into the heavens. For the Huichol, Wirikuta is the place where earth and sky join.

Asclepius, Greek god of healing, travelled to Mount Pelion in Thessaly to receive instruction in healing plants. Even today, locals list over 1,000 healing herbs in the pastures of Mount Pelion[7]. However, Asclepius used more than herbs in his treatments. Patients dreamed of their cures in special dreaming chambers where spirits visited them at night – a reminder that we must always consider the spiritual when working with the physical. This is especially true of plants.

You may never have picked a plant for use in healing, but you have probably picked flowers, even if only to make a daisy chain. As we shall see, flowers also have much to offer the shaman and provide another opportunity to harvest both plant and spirit.

85

FLOWERS

The woman stands beside a bowl of water deliciously scented with an infusion of flowers the Shipibo *payé* prepared earlier. The *payé* takes a scoop of water and pours it over the woman's head, then blows smoke as the water runs across the woman's body, falling into a puddle that drains into the river beyond. Again and again, the *payé* pours water, the power of the flowers restoring harmony and balance.

FLOWER BATHS

In order to prepare someone for the visions they might receive as part of an ayahuasca ceremony, or to bless the body afterwards so that the effect of the visions remains, Shipibo-Conibo *payé* of the Amazonian basin of Peru offer participants *baños florales*, or flower baths, where water infused with flower essence is poured over the person's head[1]. Blowing smoke and sometimes perfume across the body aids the process of cleansing. *Baños florales* are also used as a part of shamanic healing. The gentle essence of the flowers soothes the body and restores its balance. Among the Semai of Borneo, an agricultural people living around the main mountain chain of the island, *pawing* undergo *muh baunga,* or flower baths, as part of their initiation[2]. These soothe body and soul to allow *pawing* to meet the spirits of the land.

Try *baños florales* or *muh baunga* yourself, either by gathering flower petals in a sacred manner, or by using flower essences (perhaps as aromatherapy oils). Either bathe in your bathroom or take a bowl outside and pour water over your body. You will find that different flowers have different effects[3]. Some are revitalizing (such as tree blossoms), whereas others are soothing (such as lavender and rose). Try a variety and decide which works best for you.

PETAL POWER

In Uto-Aztec languages (spoken by indigenous people of Central America), metaphor and imagery relate spiritual power to flowers, and a flower itself represents spirit[4]. Early contact with Jesuit priests caused syncretization within practices of the Rarámuri shamans of Mexico (*owirúame*), and the cross became the most important healing item. However, during rituals *owirúame* ask not for a cross but a *sewáchari*, or sunflower. Again, a flower represents power.

Flowers are nodes on the web of life where power is concentrated. They are not only visually alluring, but have additional properties: a bunch offered in apology improves mood, a bouquet given to a hospital patient hastens healing, and wreaths left on graves may assist the dead to cross to the afterlife. You probably rely on the power of flowers already, but to deepen this relationship, journey to the spirit of a flower and ask for its help as an ally. You may want to explore the folklore of flowers in the region where you live and see if traditional tales provide any information that might reflect old shamanic knowledge.

TIME AND BALANCE

Flowers provide a natural means of measuring time, because they open with the first rays of dawn and close with the gathering dusk. Carl Linnaeus, the great 18th-century Swedish botanist who laid the foundation of binomial nomenclature, formulated a clock that indicated time purely through the opening and closing of flowers[5]. It started with goat's beard, which opened at 3.00am, and ended with the day lily, which closed at 8.00pm. Although plants display a regular circadian rhythm, latitude, weather and other conditions made this clock very variable. Nonetheless, many botanical gardens have since tried to recreate Linnaeus's clock and it remains a way of counting time that is natural, harmonious and profoundly beautiful.

Another scientist, Edward Bach (who, despite his Welsh ancestry, pronounced his name to rhyme with "thatch"), believed that the dew he found clinging to flower petals in the early morning contained an essence of the healing power of the flower. From this simple premise, Bach created Flower Remedies, each providing a miniscule amount of flower material in a mix of alcohol and water[6]. The amount is just enough to contain the vibrational imprint of the flower, in much the same way that homeopathic medicine works.

The remedies seem to excel in improving mood and reducing anxiety. Bach believed they restored harmony to body and soul, increasing good energy while washing out the bad. The effect sounds very similar to that of the Shipibo-Conibo *baños florales*.

Many health-food shops and pharmacies stock Bach Flower Remedies. As part of your work with flowers, you could try one or more of the range. If you do, journey to the spirit of the plant first and obtain its guidance, so that you are working not only with the physical essence of the flower but also with its spirit.

Another way in which flowers can restore balance is through a *limpia*[7]. This is performed by *curanderas* and *curanderos* (female and male healers respectively) throughout South and Central America. An object, in this case flowers, is rubbed all over a patient's body to extract bad energy and then buried where it can no longer do harm. As with *baños florales*, the healer also blows smoke over the patient so that good energy flows into the body to replace the bad. In a way, the ritual is a *baño floral* without the water.

Many other plants are suitable for healing, as we shall explore on pages 88–9, but flowers are particularly good at brightening mood and dispelling negativity. If you have a garden, or even just a window box, then you can have flowers — a soothing presence in your life, restoring its harmony and balance.

HEALING HERBS

The Mapuche shaman sings as she prepares her healing herbs. At the end of every monotonous line she adds a shrill wail, just as the spirits taught her. Through her voice she draws out the power of the plant spirits and drives away malevolent entities. Herbs are at the centre of her world, representing both who she is and the world she inhabits.

HEALING WITH HERBS

Mapuche *machis* of southern Chile use entheogens (see pages 74–7) in their rituals, including a narcotic infusion of taique plants, which have spiny leaves and beautiful red and yellow tubular flowers. Herbs with no psychoactive properties are also used to heal ailments. The *machis* prepare their herbs in a sacred manner, singing songs taught by the spirits[1]. Shamans always engage a plant's spirit as well as its physical properties.

Using herbs to heal is very common in shamanic communities. The knowledge of herbs inherited by the Igbo *dibïa* of Nigeria is part of their family lineage. Herbal remedies, *ögwü*, contain not only the physical herb but also the beliefs and cosmology of the community[2]. By submitting to treatment, a patient accepts the physiological, psychological, social and cosmological dimensions of healing – in other words, he or she is incorporated back into the established order of society. *Dibïa* treat *dis-ease*, not disease. In South Africa, *sangoma* healers gather a huge

variety of healing herbs, keeping them in a goatskin bag. They also gather modern chemicals, such as those found in cleaning products. For a *sangoma*, everything can heal if used in the right way[3]. With the forced slave migrations, knowledge of herbs travelled to the Americas, where Voudou priests (*houngan* if male and *mambo* if female) use a wide range of herbs for healing and magic. Like their African counterparts, they use artificial substances to supplement plant ingredients and offer formulas such as Waste-away Tea and the famous Love Potion Number Nine[4].

Tibetan shamanism differentiates between the "gentle" action of herbs and the "fierce" action of more invasive treatment like acupuncture. However, the effects of some herbs, such as entheogens, can be anything but gentle, so always check the safety of a herb thoroughly before you use it. Before you prepare a crop, journey to the spirit of the plant and ask if there is any particular way you should treat it (you might, like the *machis*, find the spirit gives you a song to draw out the herb's power). The easiest way of preparing a herb, if you are not drying it for storage, is to make an infusion by adding boiling water, possibly blending one herb with others. A sure way of imbibing its spirit is to make drinking the infusion a ritual. In Japanese tea ceremonies, for example, every stage obeys strict protocol so that the ritual becomes a meditation centred not on drinking tea but on finding balance and harmony in the world. It is a form of spiritual healing.

In many parts of the world, medicine is provided by the hedgerow, but this is not true for us in the West. The enormous pharmaceutical industry seems the antithesis to traditional healing, and yet this is not how shamans view it. Nähñu shamans of Mexico readily use both traditional and modern medicine. Their purpose is to heal their patients, not adhere to some image of tradition. Whatever herbal remedy we might use, we should not overlook modern medicine. If a doctor prescribes tablets for you – perhaps antibiotics for an infection – journey to the medicine's spirit and try to befriend it. That way, it will work on a spiritual as well as a physical level.

MANY USES

There are ways to use herbs, other than ingesting them[5]. Shamans from Java (*dukun*) use herbs in ritual baths. As you did with flowers, try adding herbs or their concentrated essence, to your bath. Many herbal essences are available as aromatherapy oils. When you lie in the bath, journey to the spirit of the plant and let it embrace you through its delicious aroma.

Rai shamans of Nepal (called *jhãkrī*, among other names) have a ritual similar to *limpia* (see page 87), in which a banana sapling is used to remove negative energy[6]. At midnight, during an all-night healing ritual, the *jhãkrī* ties the family hosting the ceremony to the sapling with cotton thread, moving negative influences along the thread into the sapling. Finally, with fierce drumming and yelling, the *jhãkrī* severs the thread and destroys the sapling.

Some plants are put to ordinary use by shamans. For example, the Amazonian *payé* adds kana fruit to an ayahuasca brew, not to bring any particular spiritual quality to it but to lessen the ayahuasca's bitter taste. However, in other situations kana is revered. The *payé* hands out the heart-shaped fruit to newborns, strung into a necklace symbolizing the many hearts of the baby's lineage. By blowing the power of the fruit into the baby with his or her breath, the *payé* connects the newborn's heart with all the other hearts within the community, both living and ancestral.

However you work with herbs, always remember that you draw on their spiritual as well as physical properties. The Andean Incas of Peru give three perfect coca leaves in *kint'u* offerings to the mountain gods, to Mother Earth and to each other. Encapsulated in the three coca leaves are the beliefs of the people. Putting each leaf into your mouth is to absorb and embody their power, letting it cleanse your body and soul with a wave of healing. Like the Inca, allow herbs to lie at the centre of your shamanic life, representing both who you are and the world you inhabit.

89

INCENSE

· ·

The Pharaoh Queen stands at the docks, watching the ships disgorge their precious cargo. They have returned from the first trading expedition Egypt has ever made to the land of Punt. Gold, ivory and cattle leave the ships' holds until, at last, comes the treasure the Queen has been waiting for. Thirty-one small trees, their roots held in woven baskets, are carried to the wharf, slung between poles. The Queen smiles. She will have a ready supply of myrrh from these trees, and be able to capture and harness for herself the power of its scented smoke.

THE ANCIENT WORLD

Hatshepsut (who probably died in 1457 BCE) was the only female to take the trappings of a male ruler, including a false beard, and rule Egypt as a pharaoh. Initially taking power as regent for her stepson, Thutmose III, she effectively ruled in a one-sided but not, apparently, antagonistic partnership with him[1]. Hatshepsut's reign began with the usual wars to consolidate her power. These did not last long and she soon revealed that her real enthusiasm was trade. Mounting one of the first expeditions to Punt, a land south of Egypt that has never been satisfactorily identified, her ships returned full of treasure, the most valuable items being myrrh trees. Hatshepsut had these living specimens planted in her mortuary complex at Deir el Bahri, where she also engraved images of the

expedition. This is the first known transplanting of trees in history, and it took place to obtain the resin of the tree for burning. Myrrh was known to the ancient Egyptians as the scent of the gods.

The Greek historian Plutarch (c. 46–120 CE), in a speech entitled "On the Worship of Isis and Osiris" (an essential source of information on Egyptian religious rites), notes that the ancient Egyptian temple priests burned different scents at different times of day, using frankincense at dawn and myrrh at midday[2]. These two resins retained their importance throughout antiquity and the Magi gave both to Christ at the Nativity. At dusk priests burned *kyphi*, an incense mixture first described in the Pyramid Texts as the scent the Pharaoh would enjoy in the afterlife. There seem to have been several recipes for the perfect blend of *kyphi*, all including wine, honey and raisins. Plutarch also mentions 16 other ingredients, of which only cinnamon, cassia bark, cypress, sweet flag, cedar, juniper berry, and resins and gums such as frankincense, myrrh, benzoin resin, labdanum and mastic are recognizable today. Whatever the additional unknown ingredients, it is clear that the mix would have produced a delicious and heady scent.

▶ **Burning incense sticks** are arranged in brass pots outside a temple in Hanoi, Vietnam, as a means of purifying the precinct and honouring the Buddha.

BURNING INCENSE

• •

Try making your own incense from combinations of bought or found ingredients, such as resin, berries and flowers. Many outlets supply small charcoal blocks with a round hollow that are ideal for burning incense, but putting your mix on any hot surface will cause it to burn.

92

1. Before burning your incense, offer your ingredients to the spirits of the four directions (north, south, east and west), holding them up to each quarter.

2. Say a few words dedicating the scented smoke to help yourself or others.

3. Light your charcoal block and, when it is red hot, drop your incense onto its surface. What you are after is a slow smoulder that produces smoke rather than a rapid burn.

4. Once you have your incense alight, imagine the power of the scent radiating out around the world, and then bathe in its deliciously scented smoke.

5. When the smoke dies down, add more incense until the space around you is filled with its heady aroma.

EXPERIMENTING WITH SCENTS

Although incense sticks give out a wonderful aroma and are readily available to buy, the best incense is mixed by hand[3]. You could even try gathering your own ingredients, perhaps by collecting tree resin from a forestry plantation (where regular pruning causes the sap to flow). Look for broken branches or chipped bark where sap has hardened to resin. Some wood is highly scented, so experiment with twigs you find on the ground. Berries, such as those from juniper, make a wonderful scented smoke, and you can also burn flowers, such as lavender heads, to provide a delicate aroma. Remember to ask permission from the spirit of the tree or plant before you gather anything, and make a note of your impressions of the scent each produces.

Ingredients that you cannot easily gather, such as frankincense and myrrh, can be bought online where you will also find an array of other delights to tempt you. If you burn each ingredient separately, noting its characteristics, you can then try creating your own mixture. Like a perfumer, include top notes of citrus or flowers and contrast these with base notes of resins or wood. You might even try to resurrect the aroma of the pharaohs using some of the ingredients of *kyphi*.

SCENT IN CEREMONY

In ancient Egypt, frankincense and myrrh were key ingredients in the process of mummification. The bandages that encircled a mummy dripped in oils and resins, so that the afterlife became a deliciously sweet-scented place. The aroma provided a gateway through which the spirit of the dead person moved. You can also use incense, not to reach the afterlife but to reach the otherworld. Follow the scented smoke as it drifts upward and see where it takes you. Some scents, such as the cannabis seeds the ancient Scythian shamans burned at funeral rituals, may even speed a spiritual voyager along the way[4]. (Whenever you burn anything, indoors or outside, do be careful of the fire risk.)

Incense accompanies religious and purification ceremonies the world over. In the Catholic Church, incense is used in memory of the Magi's gift at the nativity. In Korea, the dances of the shamans (*mudang*) always take place with incense burning on the altar. Maya *h'men* of Central America have always relied on the scent of burning copal to cleanse people and places before rituals. If you want to clear a space from negative energies, perhaps one that you have identified in your home (see page 10), moving burning incense through the area can work well. You might even want to obtain some copal to do this[5].

Many traditional people offer smoke to the gods or spirits. Dukha people, living in the high mountain forests in the north of Mongolia, often have to move their herds of reindeer from one grazing site to another. Before leaving a place, they gather branches of mountain juniper and leave them smouldering on a plank of larch as an offering of gratitude to the spirits of their camping site for watching over them[6]. You might also want to dedicate your incense to a particular spirit – perhaps your power animal, guardian spirit or the spirit of your sacred place.

Incense is also central to many healing rituals. Nähñu shamans of Mexico hold a burning censor before images of their helping spirits, allowing the spirit to move into the smoke, and then bring the censor next to their patient. Through the movement and intensity of the scented smoke, the spirit will reveal the nature of the illness to the shaman. Rarámuri *owirúame* from Mexico bathe their patients in the smoke of cedar wood in order to purify them and aid their healing. Native American people use a ritual they call "smudging" to do the same, blowing scented smoke over individuals to cleanse and purify them, sometimes using different ingredients to perform different functions[7]. While you might like to use cedar to purify yourself and others, you could also journey to the spirit of each ingredient you have and find out for yourself what is most appropriate for each task. As you journey with the scent of your incense, reflect on all that you have found out about plants, from meeting their spirits in tiny seeds to the lessons you have learned through planting, growing and harvesting them. While entheogens can be used to connect you to the sacred, all plants have spirits that can help you on your shamanic path. From the trees of the forest to the flowers of the hedgerow, plants are at the heart of the shamanic world. By mixing and burning the plants you gather, you can now capture and harness for yourself the power of their scented smoke.

CEREMONY AND RITUAL

The tent shakes violently as the spirits descend into the darkened interior. They pour in under the edges and through the flap of the door, whistling and murmuring as they brush past people's heads and bodies, making their presence felt. When the tent shakes so fiercely it almost collapses, a young man puts a question to the spirits, and the shaman waits for the spirits to whisper the answer in his ear. Through him, all present will draw on the wisdom of the otherworld, feeling the true power of ritual.

SPIRIT COMMUNICATION

Among the Ojibwa people of the northeastern North American woodlands, the *jiisakiiwigaan* is a tent used for communicating with the spirits[1]. After purification, the shaman (*jiisakiiwinini*) summons the spirits for questioning by those present, and he interprets their responses, sometimes using normal language and sometimes the language of the spirits. Lakota people of the plains of the United States have a similar ritual they call *yuwipi*, in which the shaman

96

is tied in a blanket at the start of the ritual[2]. By its end, with the help of the spirits, the shaman is free.

The purpose of any ritual is to give form to something that is formless — in this case, the spirits. Early anthropologists called the *jiisakiiwigaan* the "conjurer's tent", and dismissed it as a sleight of hand for a gullible audience. But this was to miss the point. The spirits were there regardless of the shaking tent; it merely provided the setting for the ritual's real aim: communicating with the spirits. Anthropologists often concentrate on the outward manifestation of a ritual, without grasping its real significance.

Ritual is a cloak worn around a sacred act[3]. It is the drama that shifts awareness so that the true work can begin. Sometimes, the more impressive the ritual is, the deeper the resulting connection to the spirits. In Malaysia, Malay shamans (*bomoh*) are often performers in shadow puppet plays or even operas, and use music, movement and recitation in their rites[4]. Among the Meitei of Manipur in India, female shamans (*maibis*) perform ritualized theatre that is the people's oldest form of performance[5]. Theatre began as a sacred means of calling upon the spirits. It was a ritual forming a

◀◀ *Black Magic (Magique Noir)*, painted by the Haitian artist and Voudou priest Hector Hyppolite, *c.* 1946–7.
◀ **Shadow puppet play** in Kotah Bharu, Malaysia. Performers often use their dramatic skills in shamanic rituals.

portal to the otherworld, allowing participants and the spirits to cross from one to the other.

When creating your own ritual (see page 98), always bear in mind what you want to achieve. Before starting, formulate your intention, just as you do before you journey to the otherworld. Do you want to empower your shamanic tools, give thanks for a harvest you have gathered, or just talk to the spirits? Make sure all your ritual is focused on this central purpose[6].

Decide next where to hold your ritual — your home might be appropriate, or you might require more room. To demarcate the space and keep power in and negativity out, many people cast a circle, inscribing it around them in the earth if they are outside, or tracing an imaginary circle on the ground if inside. Always cast in a sunwise direction, in harmony with the flow of the natural world. An altar at the centre of the space can be used for candles, incense and any tools. You may want to adorn the altar and the ritual space with natural decorations, representations of your personal spirits, or anything else that adds to the atmosphere. Create an environment that indicates to your subconscious mind that something special is about to happen.

Rituals may be long, complex and involve many people, or they may be short, personal and part of your everyday routine. Experiment with different approaches; you are sure to find aspects that allow you to feel the true power of ritual.

A SAMPLE RITUAL

These instructions form the basis of a ritual that you can easily adapt and personalize for you alone or for several participants.

1. Decide on your intention for the ritual and what you hope to achieve. If you want to cast a circle to contain your work, do so sunwise. Purify yourself and your surroundings by burning incense, blowing smoke over yourself and any others present. Walk around the space that you have demarcated for the ritual, banishing negativity and inviting positive energy to take its place.

2. Now turn to the four directions and call upon the guardians of each of these realms, asking them to protect you as you work. Drum, sing or speak to them, waiting until you really feel their presence before continuing.

3. Next, call upon your personal spirits — all those beings you usually work with, including your power animal. Ask them to join you and tell them what you hope to achieve. See the web of life stretching out from your sacred space to encompass all things in this world and the otherworld. Situate yourself at the centre of this moving network of power that you will draw upon in your work.

4. When the spirits are present, your real work can begin as you fulfil your intention for the ritual. For most rituals this will include an interaction with the spirits, perhaps even a journey to the otherworld. It can be very powerful to sing or act out these journeys as a form of sacred theatre, especially if there are other participants. Be aware of the flow of power held within your space, and take from it what you need.

5. When you have accomplished your intention, give thanks to those spirits who you called upon and who have been present throughout the rite. Thank each in turn and release them back to their own realms by telling them that the ritual is over. Give thanks to yourself, too, and express gratitude for your life.

6. When the spirits have gone, close your sacred space by extinguishing your incense and candles. If you inscribed a circle, release it by tracing the same shape in the opposite direction. Visualize any excess power spreading out in all directions and make this your offering to the world.

7. Put away your sacred tools and any temporary decorations. Feel your space revert to being normal again, just as you do the same.

8. If you feel you need extra grounding at this point, reach down and touch the earth, as the Buddha did following enlightenment. Eating something can also help.

EVERYDAY SACRED

Upon waking, the Okinawan shaman makes her way to the hearth, the centre of her home and of her life. She lights a fire in a small stone censor, praying to the fire spirit (*hintu-kan*). She gives thanks for the day, asks for protection for her family, and then puts questions to the spirit that he will take to the gods for answers. She starts every day the same way, bringing the sacredness of the spirits to her everyday life.

RITUALS FOR DAILY LIFE

The shamanism of Okinawa, the largest island in the Ryukyu chain off Japan, is distinct from that of both China and the main islands of Japan[1]. Women take the lead in almost all spiritual matters, including the role of shaman (*yuta*). The relationship between the *yuta* and the *hintu-kan* is tremendously important. Before ancestor worship, people prayed to the *hintu-kan* at a hearth of three flat stones. Today, the *yuta* (and, indeed, every senior woman in a household) still pray to the *hintu-kan*, at a ceramic censer (*kouro*). The purpose of the ritual is unchanged: to ask the *hintu-kan* to intervene with the gods on behalf of the people.

The Mongolian woman we saw sprinkling milk outside her dwelling (see page 28) starts every day with the same ritual. Like other Kalkha Mongols (the largest group in Mongolia), she offers the freshest milk to the cardinal directions, to the earth and to Munkhe Hucher Tengri, the Eternal Blue Heavens.

The nine holes in the spoon used to sprinkle the milk represent the nine layers of the otherworld[2]. The ritual brings together all aspects of the Kalkhas' world, and connects them to the otherworld, in one simple act. This is the key to everyday rituals — they need to be simple yet meaningful.

If you do not already have a ritual with which you begin the day, you might like to start performing one[3]. You could go outside, like the Kalkha Mongols, and speak your words to the directions; or you could stay indoors, like a Okinawan *yuta*, and offer prayers before your hearth or altar. Use a form of words that has special resonance for you and offer thanks for the day. Ask the spirits — including those you work closest with, such as your power animal — to watch over you, your family and friends, and ask for help with anything specific you may be facing that day.

Your preparation need not be elaborate, but remember to observe the various stages of ritual. Before you start, make sure you have a clear intention for the ritual, and set aside a special space in which to perform it. Take a few moments to centre and purify yourself, perhaps by lighting a candle or burning some incense. Then call upon the spirits. After you have interacted with them in a useful way, express your gratitude and close the ritual so that it is clear it has ended. You may spend no more than two or three minutes in total

on the ritual, but by considering each stage you will ensure that your actions always remain sacred and do not become another routine chore. If you feel your words becoming stale, then change them.

You can also mark other times of the day with short rituals, such as before you set out from home, when you arrive at work, or at certain times such as midday. The Maya people of Central America compare the midday sun to an eagle high in the sky, before it plunges to the horizon and becomes the jaguar-sun through the night. Connect to the myths and traditions of your own lands and make these the backdrop to your rituals.

The Western world differs from shamanic societies in our exclusion of the sacred from everyday tasks. Traditional people put sacredness at the heart of every activity. Next time you have to do something

▲ **Natural metaphors** lend extra meaning to ritual; for the Maya, midday is represented by an eagle-sun that plunges to the horizon at dusk, to become the jaguar-sun of night.

mundane, remember the sacred, honour the spirits and see if your life is any easier as a result.

Gratitude is also something that often seems missing in the Western world. The focus of our society is on individual rights rather than on individual responsibilities. This needs to change and the next pages show how. By acknowledging the presence of the spirits in your daily activities, you will naturally feel more grateful and more empowered as a result. Small regular rituals, like the bedtime ritual described opposite, are also a way of bringing the sacredness of the spirits to your everyday life.

A Ritual For Bedtime

Every night, as you turn off the lights, you might like
to repeat these words, possibly adapting them to reflect
your personal spirit guides. "Smooring" is an old term
describing smothering the flames of a fire and banking
up the embers so that they smoulder until dawn.

*I smoor the fire this night
As the Son of Mary would smoor it;
The compassion of God be on my fire,
The compassion of God on all my household.*

OLD CELTIC BLESSING

As you go to sleep, ask the spirits to watch over you and
to help you in resolving anything that troubles you. Finally,
reflect on six events in the day that left you feeling grateful,
so that positive thoughts surround you as you fall asleep.

MAKING OFFERINGS

The Andean shaman kneels before the sheet of white paper and begins to assemble his *despacho*. He breathes prayers into flowers, placing them at the corners of the paper. Other items follow: seeds, shells, dried fruit, candles, incense and sweets. Finally, he lays down a llama foetus, then folds the paper into a neat bundle and ties it with string. A hole awaits the offering, a gift to Pachamama, the mother of all. This sacred act reveals the shaman's innermost feelings and presents them to the spirits in gratitude.

SHOWING GRATITUDE

The Q'ero, a people of Incan descent who live high in the mountains of Peru, retain many shamanic beliefs of their ancestors. The *despacho* ceremony, in which an offering is made to Pachamama, the Earth goddess, can take hundreds of forms, but usually involves the shaman (*paq'o*) laying out offerings before tying them into a bundle and either burning or burying it[1]. The *despacho* weaves strands of sacredness into everyday existence. Each addition to the bundle represents an aspect of Q'ero belief; the llama foetus, for example, stands for the spark that gives rise to highest potential.

The purpose of any offering is, like a ritual, to give form to something that is formless — in this case our prayers and gratitude. Like the contents of a *despacho* bundle, whatever we offer to the spirits is an embodiment of our innermost thoughts, magnifying them and carrying them to the otherworld[2]. It follows, therefore, that what we give is far less important than how we give it.

Whether making your offering is a ritual in itself or included as part of a longer ceremony, always prepare as you would for any other rite. First, determine the purpose of your offering. Chinese shamanism holds that we maintain harmony between this world and the otherworld by making offerings to the spirits[3]. Misfortune results if these are neglected, but offerings of food, drink and shelter restore harmony and balance. People are not bribing the spirits but including them in their lives; offerings strengthen connection. Your offerings can also acknowledge the role of the spirits in your life.

Although Thailand is a Buddhist country, people still remember the spirits and whenever they take anything from the natural world, they usually offer something in return[4]. For example, when trees are cleared to build houses, people give offerings and construct a shrine as an alternative abode for the spirits, who once safeguarded the forest and now safeguard the community. Whenever you take, especially from the natural world, always give

▶ **Chac Mool at Chichén Itzá**, Mexico, is one of a number of similar Mayan statues that may have been sited inside temples as receptacles for sacrificial offerings.

something in return, even if it is only words of thanks that express what is in your heart.

In Mongolia people erect elaborate pyramid shrines (*obo*), made of birch poles, stones and horse skulls, at the top of mountain passes. Passing travellers, who may not even know the name of the local spirit, leave small offerings, such as cigarettes, coins and silk scarves that catch the wind, giving thanks for the spirit's protection as they cross the mountain[5]. You can also give thanks to the spirits that watch over you; it does not matter if you do not know their identity, just trust that the spirits will notice your gift.

Offerings can take many forms and blood sacrifice is common among traditional communities. The Hmong *txiv neeb* of Thailand and Laos, for example, offer the blood of a sacrificed chicken or pig during healing ceremonies. The ancient Maya believed that humans were created from the blood of the gods and that they must offer human blood in return to maintain the sacred covenant[6]. While some royal Maya caused themselves to bleed by passing the spines of a stingray through their tongue or penis, others offered the lives of captives instead. Even today, in the *yuwipi*

▲ **Huichol offering bowl**, decorated with coloured glass beads forming images of sacred animals and plants.

rite of the Lakota people, women cut flesh from their arms and offer it to the spirits in small cloth bundles.

Whatever your offering is, it must be meaningful. A Huichol *mara'akame* initiate sticks beaded models of his or her world to the inside of a gourd bowl to form a portal to the otherworld[7]. This portal allows the offering placed in the bowl to reach the spirits. Burning your offering, burying it, letting it fly in the wind, pouring it into water or simply leaving it on your altar are all ways of ensuring that it reaches the spirits. If you have nothing to offer but your prayers, then speak them with honesty, or sing them sincerely. You can also write down your thanks, burning or burying the paper so that they reach the spirits. The Lakota people hold sacred ceremonies ("giveaways") in which wealth and gifts pass among the community. Donating some of your belongings to charity can also be a sacred act.

Whatever you offer, make it with no expectation of receiving anything in return. If you ask for the protection of the spirits, for example, they have no obligation to respond, nor should you expect them to. But if you walk with authenticity and beauty, they almost certainly will. Making an offering must be a humble, sacred act that reveals your innermost feelings and presents them to the spirits in gratitude.

104

CLOTHING YOUR POWER

· ·

The shaman retires to her yurt to don her ritual costume. First, a floor-length padded robe in bright blue, decorated with appliqué. Next, a large brass mirror, hung about her neck. Then a cape, its tassels tumbling down her back in colourful streams. A fringed hat covers her head and face, its bells ringing freely. Finally, she takes a headdress of antlers, each tied with blue silk. The shaman calls down the spirits as she places the antlers upon her head, asking them to give power and strength to her ritual clothes.

DRESSING FOR RITUAL

Each element of the elaborate costume of Buryat shamans has a role in protecting and assisting the shaman during rituals, and no two costumes are alike[1]. Demonstrating the presence of spirits, the fringes and bells animate the costume, which is also adorned with images of power animals and other important spirits, often crafted from metal. A mirror (*toli*) provides protection from negative influences, reflecting any baleful stare back upon its originator. The antlers (*orgay*) represent the spirit of the deer, providing speed in the otherworld as well as good hunting. The shaman's face is covered as protection, particularly when journeying to the land of the dead; if the spirits of death do not recognize the shaman, they will not come looking afterwards. (The Evenki costume has a useful back-strap that allows an assistant to pull the shaman back to the land of the living.) The costume is a vital aspect of shamanic power, and without it Buryat shamans would not dare to interact with the spirits. An Evenki shaman (*saman*) of northern Siberia, who lost his costume to anthropologists in the 18th century, lost all his powers as a result[2].

Evenki shamans have different costumes for journeying to the upper- or lowerworld, while the *angakkuq* of Greenland have different costumes for different tasks, such as the *kila*, a coat used only for divination[3]. The shaman holds the *kila* while the community ask questions. If the answer is "no", the spirits enter the *kila* and the coat becomes heavy; if it remains light, the answer is "yes". Oroqen shamans (*saman*) of China indicate seniority with the number of tines on their antler headdress, just as real deer do[4].

In Korea, when *mudang* perform the dance of the spirits, they change their costume many times to reflect the spirits they embody[5]. Underneath, the *mudang*, if female, wears the clothes of a man, and (exceptionally) if male, wears the clothes of a woman. This gender disguise allows the shaman to embody both male and female spirits. In Thai rituals, spirit mediums, who are often peasant in origin, also don spirit attire – the clothes of traditional noblemen. Again rules are reversed in the otherworld and mediums of the lowest standing usually embody the noblest spirits.

Mudang costumes reside in dedicated shrines when not in use, and people leave offerings of food, cloth or money to honour the spirits that inhabit the clothes. Occasionally, an individual (usually a woman) may donate a new costume, embroidering her name on the fabric so that it remains close to the spirit.

In Tibet, many monasteries have an oracle that combines elements of Bon shamanism with Buddhist ritual[6]. During a séance, to signify the important moment when the spirits arrive, the medium ties a piece of red cloth around his head and dons a headdress, adding to the spectacle and indicating that ordinary reality has given way to something sacred.

CHOOSING YOUR COSTUME

Wearing ordinary clothes to journey to the otherworld may have left you feeling unprepared, even exposed. If so, consider making your own shamanic costume. Certainly, for many traditional shamans the very act of putting on a costume shifts their awareness and prepares the soul for its journey to the otherworld. You might even want to have several costumes, perhaps to represent different aspects of your practice.

Your costume can be as elaborate as those of the Buryat shamans, or as simple as you desire. A female shaman of the western Siberian Teleutians wears only

◀ **Costumes embodying spirits** worn by the Makuna tribe of Colombia in an annual dance in which animals spirits are offered food in exchange for the animals humans will kill.

a cap (*astyuchke*) while journeying to the otherworld[7]. Chepang shamans (*pande*) from the poor central southern area of Nepal wear just two necklaces when they journey[8]. You might want to hang power objects and other amulets onto your costume, for protection and to attract helping spirits. The talismans of the Yakut shamans of eastern Siberia are metal, so one of their costumes can weigh close to 40lb (18kg)![9]

Not all shamanic costumes become imbued with power. The clothing of the Hmong *txiv neeb* of Thailand and Laos, for example, includes a face-covering fringe like that worn by Siberian shamans, but the outfit is part of the setting for shamanic ritual, rather than an embodiment of power[10]. This is an important reminder that we should never become too reliant upon a costume – or any other shamanic tool for that matter. If we are unable to work without certain paraphernalia, we have abdicated our responsibility and power to those objects. Special clothes may provide a shortcut in shamanic work, but should not be the only route we follow in order to connect with our power.

Whether you wear ritual clothing or not is up to you. There may be a time when the spirits give you a costume in the otherworld and you feel bound to re-create it in this world. In Siberia, many shamans first see their costume in a dream; if you do, consider whether the costume is to attract and embody power or is simply a stage prop. If you need help and advice, journey to your spirit guides and ask them to give power and strength to your ritual clothes.

107

SONGS OF THE SPIRITS

The Sámi shaman gives voice to his *jojk*, his breath in the Arctic air a thick plume of power. His *jojk* concerns a bear and he feels its spirit come close as he gives form to the bear's shaggy coat, its razor-sharp claws, its growl. The shaman's *joik* brings the bear into being, as he calls it with the simple power of his song.

SHAMANIC VOICE

A cross between chanting and yodelling unique to the Sámi of Lapland, a *jojk* (pronounced "yoik") is a way of invoking an animal, a person or part of the natural world[1]. Eschewing all but a few words, the *jojk* comprises sounds that rise spontaneously from the heart: the sounds of animals, of the winds, of a person's innermost thoughts. The singer does not merely *jojk* about a thing, but *jojks* the thing into being – just like the shaman (*noaidi*) did with the bear. Through the *jojk*, a *noaidi* can journey to the otherworld, shapeshift into different animals or become one with the land.

A *jojk* is inherited through families or given to a *noaidi* by the spirits. This is also true for *payé* in the Amazon, who learns the songs (*icaros*) of a plant spirit (see page 76)[2]. By singing an *icaro*, the *payé* calls upon the spirit and gives voice to its power. Entheogenic plants provide visions but the *icaro* contains the wisdom of those visions. An *icaro*, like a *jojk*, helps the *payé* journey to the otherworld, by invoking the visionary effects of ayahuasca and other entheogens, and it can also be used to transfer the healing power of the *payé* to a patient. *Icaros* may be in many languages, or may be wordless whistles, but an exact rendition is required. The songs that Yuman shamans (*kusiyai*) of northern Mexico gain from dreams use a language unintelligible to anyone else, and have no power unless sung by the individuals who first dreamed them[3].

Avá-Chiripá tribespeople of the Brazilian jungle often receive individual power chants from the spirits in dreams. It is the tone of the chant that carries its power, not the words, which become progressively unintelligible[4]. Similarly, *payé* songs of the Matsigenka of south-eastern Peru are often untranslatable, gaining power through onomatopoeic rhythm.

Yaminahua *payé* in Amazonian Peru and Brazil consider songs to be their most valuable possession as they contain the essence of the shamans' power, wisdom and ability to heal[5]. The metaphorical language of the song provides a means to access this power. For the Shipibo-Conibo *payé* of Peru, illness is a broken aura, which can be sung back into completeness[6].

Songs received from bird spirits become the wings of the Akawaio *payé* of Colombia, allowing flight to the otherworld[7]. In central Africa, !Kung *n/um k"ausi* use songs about animals, or songs imitating the sounds of animals, to initiate trance[8]. The songs connect to the animal spirits, allowing the shaman to touch them. Without the song, the spirits remain out of reach.

108

Pima shamans of southern Arizona and northern Mexico do not share the events of shamanic journeys with their communities[9]. All they reveal is the songs the spirits give to them, reciting these in the spirit's voice. Some contain information or provide shamanic power; others invoke dancing among the listeners. The half-human, half-bird spirit who gives the Pima the Swallow Social Dance songs brags about its power in a way that the shaman would find unthinkable.

Pima shamans also use songs for diagnosing and healing patients. The form and even the words of the song may not differ substantially from the dancing songs, but the shaman now growls the words rather than crooning them. The songs take on a deeper significance and carry great power. The Kuna *payé* of Panama use healing songs to explain the mythological significance of illness and so deduce its likely origin.

FINDING YOUR SONG

If you have not yet received a shamanic song or chant, journey to the otherworld and ask your helping spirits to teach you one. Whether it is simple or elaborate, practise it so that you can use it whenever you want empowerment and to call your spirit allies close. Spirits enter the ears of an Evenki *saman* and whisper songs that provide protection when the *saman* is alone in the forest. Whisper your song when you feel the need for assistance.

Songs store power that a shaman releases through reciting their words. The power is carried on the shaman's breath. Among Peruvian people, *camay* is a means of breathing power into something to convey a blessing of unity[10]. The breath provides a connection between the giver and the receiver that transcends all boundaries. Fire, or water in the form of liquor, sometimes supplements the breath, but the aim is always to restore harmony and balance. Indeed, people believe that the creator, Viracocha, breathed the dream that became reality into existence in this way. You can easily share a blessing of unity with others, supplemented by the songs or chants your spirits give you.

When you have learned one song or chant to empower you and bring the spirits close, journey to receive additional songs. Perhaps there is one that accelerates the process of shapeshifting into your power animal. Many shamans use songs for diagnosing or healing illness, and while we will explore healing later (see Part VI), you might like to start gathering songs for the process. Unlike other shamanic paraphernalia, a song is constantly with you and you can call upon it anywhere. It is a direct route to empowerment, wisdom and healing. While you may go on to add music to your words, and pages 110-11 describe how you can do this, remember that you can always call the spirits with the simple power of your song.

MAKING MUSIC

The drums start to pound as the Santería ritual starts and people begin to dance. A woman in a white dress, a scarf wrapped around her head, breaks into chant, and soon the entire room reverberates to the sound. It will be some time before the first spirit descends, drawn from the otherworld by the music.

USING DRUMS AND OTHER INSTRUMENTS

Santería, or the "Way of the Saints", is centred upon Cuba but has roots in the Yoruba tradition of Nigeria, Benin and Togo[1]. The ancestral belief in spirits (*orishas*) held by slaves transported to Cuba became entwined with Catholicism and led to a distinct tradition[2], but the reliance on pulsating music, song and dance did not change and still forms the basis of Santería rituals (*bembé* in the Lakumí dialect of the Yoruba language). In *bembé* the *orishas* descend and "mount", or possess, the dancers. There is no equivalent to a shaman and the *orishas* may mount anyone present – in another inversion of this world's hierarchy, the least important member of the group may be the first choice of an *orisha*. Drumming is extremely important as each song-cycle (*oru*) relates to a particular *orisha* and the spirit moves through sound to enter and possess the mount. Without music, the *orisha* would not appear.

The drum has many uses in shamanism, from divination table to spirit-catcher, but it is its sound that carries the shaman to the otherworld. In Eurasian shamanism, the drum is referred to as a boat or a horse as it carries the shaman from one world to another. Bronze Age rock art from Lapland shows drumming shamans in upside-down boats, as if in the inverted realm of the otherworld[3]. Yakut shamans from northwestern Siberia chant "the drum is my horse" repeatedly as its sound takes them to the spirits. Among the Shor people, a Turkic group from southern Siberia, shamans make drums from deerskins, and the deer whispers its story to the shaman during the drum's first use[4]. The shaman keeps the drum for what would have been the rest of the deer's natural lifespan had it lived, then abandons it in the forest.

Drumming may predate the evolution of humans. Macaque monkeys have been shown to drum objects as social display, and chimpanzees drum on buttress roots for the same purpose. It is likely that our earliest ancestors did the same, and they possibly entered trance as a result. Perhaps the spiritual significance of drumming led to its early adoption[5]. Sumerian statues from around 2,000 BCE are the first to portray women drumming in religious rites. Simple frame drums dating to 950–700 BCE have been found in China and Egypt, and the design has not changed much since.

You may want to beat your own drum as you journey to the otherworld. This is what many Siberian shamans do, while also chanting, singing and even dancing. Before using a drum for the first time, journey to its spirit, like the Shor shamans. You may even want to make your own drum, perhaps painting its surface to depict your power animal or the drum's spirit. Manchu people of northern China believe that Abikia Hehe, the sky goddess, made the first drum and beater from a piece of the sky and a mountain. Newly initiated shamans follow her lead and make their own drum, obtaining its design and rituals for its creation through dreams[6]. An all-night ritual enlivens the drum and embodies the power of the spirits within it. If you are going to make a drum, journey first to obtain advice on its design and any rituals you should follow before using it.

In the southern European caves decorated with Ice Age shamanic visions, archaeologists have found bullroarers — perforated slats swung on a cord to produce a low roar, like the sound of a bull[7]. The Dogon of Mali still use these instruments in rituals, to represent the voice of their ancestors, while Australian Aborigines use them to scare away malevolent spirits, and west Greenland Inuit use them to drive out illness.

Ice Age hunters also made flutes, often from bird wings, that mimic the call of a bird[8]. People may have used them to journey to the upperworld or to shapeshift into a bird. Kokopelli, the flute-playing, hunchbacked spirit of the southeastern United States, embodies the spirit of music[9]. Zuni people believe that he ushers in the spring rains and ancient rock art showing his erect phallus also reveals him to be a fertility deity. Maybe his flute represented creative potential.

To call the spirits, Amazonian *payé* use panpipes, as well as bows — simple instruments with a single string pulled taut on a curved piece of wood. Tsugaru *itako* of Japan tap a bow to invoke a spirit of the dead, while a Kazakh shaman (*baqsı*) uses a *qobız*, another single-stringed instrument, to induce trance. In Tuva, shamans play mouth harps for the same reason.

You can use different instruments to help you to reach the otherworld and to bring life to your rituals Like the Santería dancers, you may find that you can interact with the spirits that inhabit the music. If a rhythm pulls you to your feet and makes you dance, the spirits will surely follow close behind, drawn from the otherworld by your music.

111

▲ **Nazca ritual drum** from Peru, decorated with a supernatural cat. It is inverted before playing.

DANCING YOUR PRAYERS

The !Kung women sit in a large circle on the packed earth of the African savannah and clap, chant and rattle a rhythmic, pounding beat. Within the circle, dancing men pound up dust, their bodies arching backward. Suddenly, one of the group, his nose dripping blood, leans over a patient on the ground, and pulls something out of her. The shaman's power is at its height, fuelled by the rhythmic intensity of the dance.

112

TRANCE DANCE

The all-night dances of the !Kung see many *n/um k"ausi* enter trance[1]. They call the rise of power "boiling" and they draw this energy from the music of the women, transmitting it through touch to each other and on to their patients. If a shaman cannot transmit energy, his system overloads and he swoons into unconsciousness.

Mevlevi dervishes of Konya in Turkey whirl in circles to initiate trance and access the realm of God; before long, they are lost to this world. Chinese shamans also use dance to initiate trance, and in Indonesia music accompanying a shaman's trance dance (*ana mata da*) often affects the audience, too,

▶ *Prayer Time*, a painting by Jamaican visionary Everald Brown (1922), shows a drumming prayer service taking place in a mystical landscape.

so that the entire room journeys to the otherworld[2]. In Niger, the music of trance dances gets faster and faster as participants circle, thumping the earth with their feet. When the spirits descend and possess dancers, the music slows. Dances like these are the source of Santería and Voudou rituals in the New World.

The complicated choreography of the Inuit *aghula* dance shifts awareness until the soul of the dancer leaves the body and journeys to the otherworld, the dancer's body still maintaining the rhythm of the dance[3]. Among Rarámuri people of Mexico, vigorous dancing by the shaman (*owirúame*) demonstrates his strength and embodies the power of the spirits[4]. The dance itself holds power. *Mudang* in Korea embody spirits through long, ornate dances, changing costume every time a new spirit arrives (see page 105). Here, men play the instruments and women dance.

Like Santería in Cuba, the Candomblé tradition in Brazil also has roots in West Africa and was brought over by slave trading[5]. Even the names of the spirts have an identical pronunciation: *orixás* and *orishas*. Voudou has similar roots, and Congo Square in New Orleans once pulsated to drums and the cries of the possessed in dances brought from Africa[6]. Each dance allowed a particular spirit (*lwa*) to cross from the otherworld and join the dance. Jazz started here.

For a different experience of the otherworld, try journeying while dancing, perhaps while also playing a drum. Try to bring forth thoughts and emotions in your dance, giving them form just as your movements

114

RAISE POWER THROUGH DANCE

• •

For this exercise, make sure you give yourself the time, space and privacy to express yourself fully.

1. Play rhythmic music in the background or beat out your own pulsating sounds on a drum.

2. As you lose yourself in the music, bring forth your thoughts and emotions. Embody your joy, your sadness, your hopes and your dreams, and feel your body move as you express your innermost feelings. The power of each feeling resides in the dance and you are now expressing and bringing forth its form.

3. You can also dance to raise the power of your spirit allies. Feel them about you and within you, and share in their unending supply of energy and power.

4. You will not be possessed (unless you give your permission to be), so raise as much power as you want, stamping your feet on the floor, banging your drum and raising your voice to the heavens. Dance embodies power.

5. When the dance ends, thank the spirits that surround you and spend a few moments bringing your body back to a standstill.

gave form to your power animal when you shapeshifted (see page 71). As you practise the exercise opposite, remember that power resides in your dance[7].

HEALING AND PROTECTION

In southern Italy a bite from a tarantula spider is thought to lead to possession known as "tarantism"[8]. Only frenzied dancing can expel the power of the spider from the sufferer's body. When women of the Kel Ewey Tuareg, a nomadic desert people, are possessed by spirits or "people of solitude", they can only be cured by all-night rituals of song and music, often accompanied by uncharacteristic sexual licentiousness[9].

The *ogichidanimidiwin* is a dance Ojibwa people perform in northeastern North America to enlist the aid of the *manitou*, the community's protecting spirits. It often takes place as part of a healing ceremony. You might like to find a dance of protection yourself. Hold an image of protection in your mind, whatever it means to you, and try to embody it in a dance. Give yourself over totally to the dance, but then, as it settles into a pattern, reduce it to two or three key steps. Later, whenever you perform them, these few steps will bring you the full power of your protection dance.

In another Ojibwa dance (the *windigokan*), dancers dress as skeleton spirits and drive out disease-causing demons through dancing, music and song. The Ainu of northern Japan also drive away demons through dance, their heavy steps and jumping adding menace to the loud cries of the participants.

The Sun Dance of plains Indians in the United States also seeks to heal, through the suffering of the dancers[10]. Going without food and drink for four days, they blow on eagle-bone whistles and pray fervently for the sick, offering their own agony as payment for healing. On the last day, dancers pierce their skin with hooks and attach themselves to a post, breaking free at the climax to the dance and showering the earth with their blood. It is a dance of awesome power.

SPIRIT JOURNEYS

In the southwestern United States, Paiute shamans dance their spirit journeys as they experience them, enabling observers to give assistance when necessary. The Malay *bomoh* also dance their journeys, as do the Manipur Meitei *maibis* in India (see page 97). You may wish to try this yourself, either alone or in front of others so they can follow your journey. You may even wish to dance your aspirations for the future. The Ghost Dance that swept Native America in the late 19th century sought a future without white exploitation, and the peaceful dance caused such terror in colonial authorities that it eventually led to the massacre of the Oglala Lakota at Wounded Knee[11]. It did not achieve its aims, but the dance still held considerable power.

However you dance, give yourself over to the moment. Let your soul soar as your movement embodies your hopes and dreams, and allow your power to reach its height, fuelled by the rhythmic intensity of the dance.

SEASONAL CELEBRATIONS

The salmon talk among themselves as they swim past the Tsugaru village under the night sky, their voices rising above the icy water. No one in the village hears. All have gathered for the midwinter feast, celebrating the return of the salmon, and not a soul must see or hear the fish pass. People will sing and dance all night, celebrating the eternal circle of life.

CONTINUITY AND CHANGE

Salmon have always been an important resource for Tsugaru people from northern Japan. The fish return upstream each winter, led by two salmon kings: Osuke ("big one"), representing the head of the salmon, and Kosuke ("little one") representing its tail[1]. The feast the villagers hold to avoid noticing their passing is just one of many traditional rituals celebrating seasonal events. They mark change, but also mark continuity, as each ritual remains the same across years and even generations. The salmon have always swum past the Tsuguru village and, if the villagers continue to stay out of sight, they always will. Such rituals connect us to the unchanging centre around which life turns.

Every midsummer's eve, shamans from Khakassia in Siberia lead people to the hills above the River Abakan[2]. Here, people light a fire and play drums, purifying their bodies. Then they descend to the river and light another fire on a raft. Prayers are placed in the fire, which is floated downstream as a gift to the Master of the Water in return for a spring free from flooding. People feed on a sacrificed sheep and, just before sunrise, follow bell-ringing shamans to the hill top, where they offer prayers to the emerging sun.

Many people watch sunrise at midsummer, such as the Druids who visit Stonehenge in England. It is the culmination of the journey from winter to summer and the midpoint of the year. If you do not do so already, mark the event with your own ritual, perhaps taking inspiration from the Khakass shamans and greeting the rising sun with your prayers and gratitude.

You can also offer thanks at harvest time. For the Manchu of China, this involves offering some of the harvest[3]. Liquid is poured into the ear of a pig; if the animal shakes its head, the spirits accept the sacrifice. The pig is killed and jointed, the meat cooked, and the animal is reassembled as a gift to the spirits. Chepang people from Nepal also offer some of their harvest to the spirits at Chhonam, an auspicious time when *pande* perform healing rituals and initiate new *pande*.

Late autumn brings Día de los Muertos, the Day of the Dead, to Mexico[4]. In this festival, dating back to Mictecacihuatl, the Aztec celebration of the goddess of the underworld, each family honours their dead, making prayers and offerings and decorating graves.

▶ **Sun Dance celebration** of the Shoshone people of the United States, depicted during the 19th century.

Little is sombre in this festival, and people revel in the spirits' closeness. The Celtic feast of Samhain is today a Druid and Wiccan equivalent to the Day of the Dead when practitioners honour their own ancestors, with Hallowe'en its commercial offshoot. This is an ideal time to remember your own ancestors in ritual.

At midwinter, "Big Heads" of the North American Iroquois, wearing buffalo skins and masks, go from house to house calling people and stirring up fire ashes as an offering to the Creator[5]. You could create your own ritual to welcome back the sun after the shortest day In Korea, the New Year is marked with "Welcoming the Drum" celebrations, which can be elaborate or just a lone individual beating a drum before a candle.

Returning spring is marked by the Chinese Oroqen people with hunting rituals and bear sacrifice[6]. Believing they are descended from the bear, they call the slain beast *yaya* (grandfather) or *taitie* (grandmother). The head is preserved for a "wind burial", in which it is suspended between two trees.

May Day comes from the Celtic festival of Beltane, when livestock is moved onto summer pastures[7]. At this time of purification, stock was driven between two fires, to smoke out insects as well as ensure protection over the coming months. This was a symbolic means of moving from the dark of winter to the light of summer.

Timeless and unchanging, these festivals also represent a crossing and moving forward — in this paradox their power rests. However you celebrate the cycle of the seasons and the year's natural events, recognize that any change you observe is transitory, and that nature herself remains unchanging[8]. Your rituals need to reflect both transformation and constancy, celebrating the eternal circle of life.

On 31 October and 1 November, Mexico is festive for the Day of the Dead. People visit graveyards to offer food, drink and marigold flowers to the dead, and altars abound with colourful, even jocular images of skulls and crosses, such as skull-shaped sweets on the graves of children.

RITES OF PASSAGE

The spirits arrive dressed in feathers and pigs' tusks. They run amok through the Orokaiva village, striking property and persons alike. They hound the terrified youngsters of the community into the forest to the sacrificial platform where pigs meet their end. On this day, each child will also meet death and become a spirit, moving beyond this world and briefly touching the sacred before being born again.

COMING OF AGE

Each child of the Orokaiva people of Papua New Guinea undergoes a dramatic ritual of death and rebirth before entering adulthood, as hunters abduct the children and enact slaying them on the sacrificial platform[1]. Once "dead", the children are blindfolded and taken to a hut in the jungle, where they remain for many days. During this time the children are taught the spiritual traditions of the people. Finally, they return to the village and re-enact their abduction, this time playing the part of the hunters. The children are now adults. The ritual concludes with the former children distributing sacrificed pig meat to the community.

We all change continuously. You are not the same person you were when you started reading this chapter and you will be different again by the end of it. Every action you take, every thought that you have, changes you. However, not every change is significant. If you look back over your life, you probably have a series of vague memories of phases in which you changed: from child to adolescent, from adolescent to adult, maybe from adult to elder. But for traditional people, each of these changes is definite, structured and definable.

Among the Ankave, forest farmers of Papua New Guinea who number no more than 1,000, boys reaching manhood are smeared with the seeds of the pandanus tree[2]. These are bright red and represent blood, the symbol of life. Areca palm nuts, however, are prohibited in initiation; they also produce a red liquid, but it dries the mouth upon chewing, and is associated with death. Thus the two trees have very different symbolism.

A *wakan kaga*, or "one who enacts a spirit being", of the Lakota people of the central plains of the United States conducts the puberty ritual for girls. Its exact details are unknown; many traditional people keep such rituals hidden from outsiders and even from non-initiates within their own community. Aboriginal people of Australia have many rituals for both boys and girls, some including stages over many years, and yet many details also remain secret. In some regions boys receive circumcision as part of entry into adulthood, and in all cases initiates learn the esoteric wisdom of the community. As with all rituals celebrating change, interaction with sacred knowledge is essential.

For the Shuar of the Amazon forests of Ecuador and Peru, *arutam* is a type of soul that a person receives not at birth but during a rite of passage held

TRANSFORMATIVE RITUAL

Each person undergoing a coming-of-age ritual outwardly moves from one state to another, either from boy to man, or from girl to woman. Inwardly, however, he or she does much more. Orokaiva children die in this world and become spirits in another. They touch the sacred and learn spiritual wisdom before returning to their community. They go through a rite of passage, a sacred ritual of three stages[3]:

1. First, the initiate dies to this world.
2. Once "dead", he or she resides in a liminal state, betwixt and between the worlds; this is when an individual can reach out to the spirits and the sacred, and when a quest for a vision of life takes place.
3. After being altered by the experience, the initiate is reborn and returns to his or her community, changed in the eyes of all.

at a sacred waterfall[4]. *Ayahuasqueros* see the *arutam* as an inverted rainbow in a man's chest; it is essential for Shuar men and, before obtaining it, they are not fully human. Among Amazonian Avá-Chiripá people, *payé* name children with a word of power obtained in trance. The name links to an individual's soul, which only becomes complete with the addition of the name. When a person is in extremity, facing certain death, a *payé* may change the individual's soul name so that if it dies, it will not take the rest of the person with it[5]. In addition to their name, boys receive a *tembetá*, an ornament worn in the lower lip. This connects the individual to Tupá, the sky god, and to his power.

CELEBRATING LIFE

In Korea, people perform rite-of-passage rituals for many occasions, including births, weddings, anniversaries, illnesses and deaths. We may also mark these occasions, but we omit a vital aspect: the

spirits and the sacred. For traditional people in Korea, childbirth does not just concern the pregnant woman and her partner. It is impossible without the help of the spirits and a *mudang* must journey to the otherworld and enlist their aid[6]. Shamans understand the liminal space that is occupied by initiates undergoing rites of passage, and they can help guide people through it.

In traditional societies, no rite of passage is complete without touching the sacred and returning a changed person. While the suffering inherent in many rites of passage, which mimic the effects of death, are inappropriate to replicate in the Western world, we ignore these rituals at our peril. Many of our young people occupy a liminal state between child and adult, but this confused, uncertain place does not usually bring them close to anything sacred. We need to bring back rites of passage and celebrate changes of state in a traditional manner, moving beyond this world and briefly touching the sacred before being born again.

121

INITIATION

As she closes her eyes, the woman knows that her children will be waiting for her. It is months since the last one died and now they haunt her dreams, calling her to accept her path. Still she resists, and her health, her sanity and even her life are slipping away. She suffers the pain of grief and is not ready for this role. In the otherworld, her children do not understand and implore their mother to heed their call, and find strength in her suffering and power in her pain.

INITIATION THROUGH SUFFERING

The call of the spirits to shamanism often entails much suffering. Spirit mediums of Hong Kong are usually women called by their deceased children[1]. If they reject the call, and most do, their behaviour becomes irrational, their speech incomprehensible, and they suffer terribly until they accept the call and recover.

Such a call generally comes in dreams. In Argentina, potential Toba shamans dream about spirits, such as NwaGanaGanaq ("owner of the palm grove"), who grants wisdom and the power to heal and harm[2]. Those who ignore such dreams will become ill and may even die. For the Semai *pawing* of Malaysian Borneo, ignoring ancestor spirits in dreams inevitably causes illness. In nearby West Kalimantan in Indonesian Borneo, the Taman know that illness induced by the spirits may travel from one part of the body to another, and that becoming a shaman (*balien*) is the only cure[3].

Traditional communities see illness and suffering as a route to shamanism[4]. For Yaka people of southwestern Congo, becoming an *ngaanga ngoombu* starts with chronic illness that is assumed to come from the mother's lineage, and allows trance and interaction with the spirits. In Thailand and Laos, Hmong *txiv neeb* begin their path with chronic illness that does not respond to traditional or modern cures, with certain afflictions, such as epilepsy, seen as particularly significant. Inuit *angakkuq* often hear the call of the spirits after serious accidents, while Hopi shamans (*povosyaqam* and other related names that describe "seeing with special eyes")

▶ **Dyak amulet** from Borneo, used to ward off enemies, bring good luck and provide healing.

suffer life-threatening illness or lightning strikes before initiation.

It is through such suffering that a shaman draws power. If you look back over your life, there will be times when you suffered either physically or emotionally. Reflect upon these and try to recall how you felt. It is likely that there was something unreal about how you were, as if part of you had slipped into another world. Many people who suffer trauma report the experience of looking at their body from outside – this is the start of a journey to the otherworld. It is through the gate of suffering that power flows and the spirits can reach us. Ignoring their call only prolongs our agony.

Power may be inherited through family lineage or from deceased ancestors. In Ghana, potential Ashanti shamans become possessed by dead *akomfo* at funerals, leading to mental and physical illness[5]. Sometimes the initiate runs into the forest, but the suffering continues. It is only when the initiate approaches a senior *akomfo* and accepts the call of the spirits that the condition subsides and training begins. Shamans of Sakha in eastern Siberia inherit their ability from shamanic ancestry, but the call still manifests as illness interpreted as acquainting the individual with suffering, death and the otherworld[6]. Among the Nong of southern China, children who may become shamans (*paq*) are identified from their birth charts, but all still suffer illness as part of their calling.

ACCEPTING YOUR CALL

A shaman's initiation follows the three stages of rites of passage (see page 121). Affliction with illness is followed by a time away from the world, listening to the spirits. To outsiders, this may appear as madness. Finally, the individual accepts the call and seeks healing and re-entry into the community as a shaman. Think whether these themes were apparent in your periods of suffering. Can you draw power and purpose from them, despite the pain you felt at the time?

The training that follows acceptance can be arduous. For a Yaka initiate, this involves nine months of seclusion under the instruction of a shaman who imparts knowledge and also gathers herbs for enemas to transform the initiate's body into a channel of spirit communication. Among the Kogi people of Columbia, initiate shamans (*mumas*) may remain in complete darkness for many years from childhood[7].

Did you acknowledge the spiritual importance of your suffering and answer the spirits' call? If not, has the suffering ever truly left you? Journey now to the spirit of your suffering and make peace. Understand that suffering is a part of your journey. By recognizing these dark times as portals to power, you can reduce, even negate, their hold over you. Give yourself over to the call of the spirits, accept the potential for light in the darkness. You have survived. Now find strength in your suffering and power in your pain.

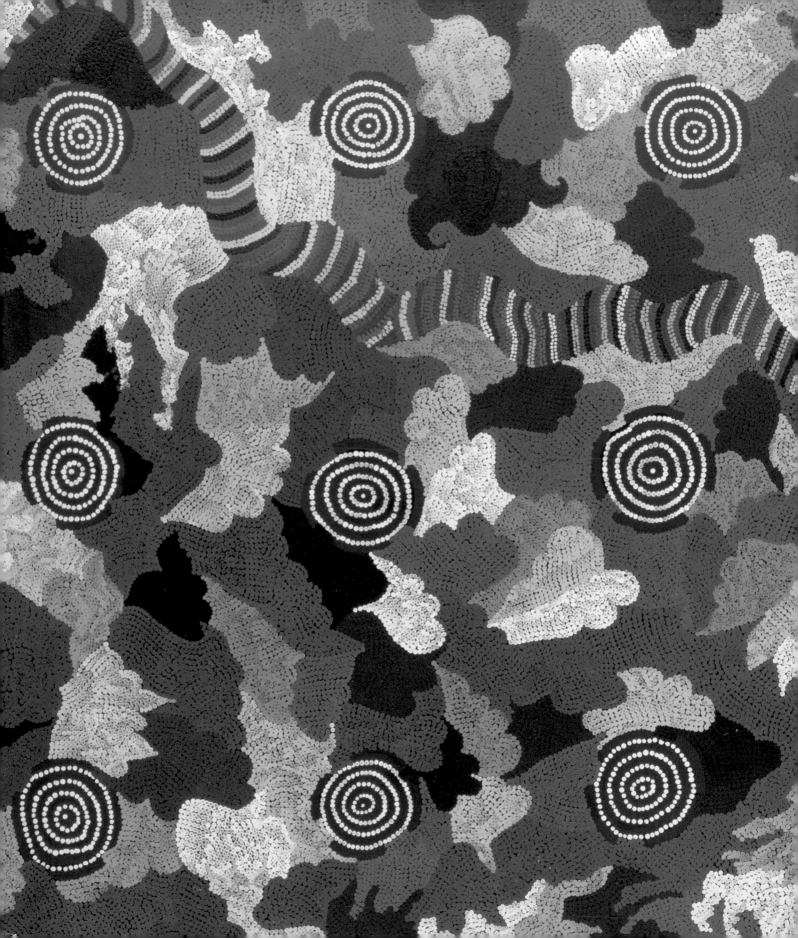

FEELING GOOD IN YOUR SKIN

Ngungi has returned changed from his travels, his lame leg and lost eye testament to the trials he encountered in his search for wisdom. Ever since his father sent the stupid, impetuous boy away, he has sought knowledge from all who would teach him. But his biggest lesson came from disfigurement, sacrificing his physical body so that his spirit might soar. Returning as a god who will serve as craftsman, he knows his power rests in his physical limitations.

DISFIGUREMENT AND DISABILITY

We have already seen (on pages 122–3) that shamans gain power through suffering. The Zulus believe that the power of Ngungi, god of blacksmithing, comes from the sacrifice of his leg and eye, made to rid himself of "stupidity", a reference to the unenlightened attitude of those who have not experienced sacred transformation[1]. The Norse God Odin underwent a similar change when he hung on Yggdrasil for nine days and nights to gain wisdom from the nine realms of the otherworld[2]. He also sacrificed an eye, to gain an ability to know all events past and future.

◀◀ *Rainbow Serpent Dreaming* (1989) by Aboriginal painter Ginger Tjakamarra and his wife, Wingie Napaltjami.
▶ **Norse god Odin**, who sacrificed an eye in return for shamanic powers, appears (at left) with Thor and Freya in this 12th-century Swedish tapestry.

When such suffering is continuous, through disability, the power it generates is magnified. Traditional communities believe that a physically or mentally disabled individual has been touched by the spirits and has great power as a result. Most of the Sakha shamans of eastern Siberia inherit their position, but a newborn with notable physical defects is thought to have been chosen by the gods to become a shaman[3]. In Peru, those born with birth defects or highly visible birthmarks are destined to become shamans, as are those born in northern Eurasia with a cowl (covered with the amniotic membrane), a single tooth (particularly in Hungary) or extra bones. Resisting such signs leads to sickness in both the child and close relatives. It is the family's responsibility to ensure that the child follows his or her destiny. For the Hmong, epilepsy is a sign of shamanic power, and autism is often viewed in the same way. When Rupert Isaacson, author of *The Horse Boy*, took his autistic son to Siberia to find healing among the shamans, they predicted that the child would become a shaman because he had already experienced the spirit world[4].

In Japan, *itako* are born blind, their lack of vision in this world increasing their ability to see into the otherworld[5]. In the *kuchiyose* divination ceremony, *itako* transmit the words of the dead, drawing language from the dark world they inhabit. In Korea, visual impairment is also a path to shamanism, and

shamans who are not blind cover their eyes to journey to the otherworld. You might want to try this, or try journeying in a darkened room with your eyes open, peering into new realms. Some shamans, such as Inuit *angakkuq* and the lead participant at the Lakota *yuwipi* ceremony, are tied before beginning the ritual. It is as if their physical restraint or impairment in this world increases their ability to act in the other, reflecting the traditional inversion of the otherworld.

We all have physical limitations, even if not at the same level as Ngungi. Whatever your imperfection, shamans consider it a source of power – proof that you are touched by the spirits. Journey to the spirit of your imperfection, just as you did with your suffering, and befriend it. Reassess any negative attitudes you have toward yourself, and allow your imperfection to remain as a sign of your calling and a gateway to your power.

MARGINALITY AND POWER

Shamanism attracts the marginalized. Burmese spirit mediums (*natkadaw*), usually women or transsexual men, are identified by their unusual physical appearance and also by their social marginality in terms of poverty and low caste[6]. By marrying a spirit lord, they can elevate their position. We have seen (page 105) that the lowest-status Thai mediums work with the most prestigious spirits, while the Nepalese Chepang people, often considered "untouchable", provide the most revered of the *pande*. Status as a spirit medium is in inverse proportion to status in society. More than simple inversion, this shows shamans drawing upon an apparent weakness for their power.

In Nigeria and Niger, successful Hausa people are increasingly turning to Islam and those who adhere to the old Bori rituals of spirit possession are predominantly women and this society's outcasts, such as the mentally ill, prostitutes, homosexuals and transvestites[7]. Shamans are people who live on the edge, through illness, disability or social exclusion.

If you ever feel disempowered in this world, it may be a sign revealing a source of power. You need to accept and open your scars for that power to flow. Draw strength from weakness and do not try to hide from the truth of your existence. Revel in who you are and what you are, and know that power rests in your physical limitations.

127

SEXUALITY IN SHAMANISM

· ·

The Mohave boy stands motionless in the circle, feeling all eyes upon him. A figure, unseen by the boy, begins a song that is full of power and slowly, led by forces outside his control, the boy begins to dance. Three more songs follow and the boy's heart soars to meet each, his dancing body unable to express fully the surge of energy within him. The tribespeople have found another *alyha*. The boy has become a girl and shamanic power flows from her gender role.

CROSSING BOUNDARIES

In the southwestern United States, Mohave boys between the ages of nine and 12 indicate at dance ceremonies their preference for initiating either as a male or as an *alyha*[1]. If they choose the path of the *alyha* by dancing to the songs, they leave the dance, bathe and change into a skirt before receiving a new, female name. Their old, male name will never be used again. Although schooling (especially the use of boarding institutions) has dented the tradition, many Native American people still recognize a third gender – often referred to by outsiders as *berdache*, "a male who fills non-male social roles"[2]. *Berdaches* exist at the heart of their communities, honoured as religious specialists.

Modern medicine has negated the existence of certain people[3]. A child born hermaphrodite (of mixed male and female sex) undergoes surgery to correct the "disorder", with parents and surgeons selecting which sex the child will become. The child is not consulted and may later feel that the surgery was an unnecessary and wrong intervention. Traditional societies left room for these individuals, perfectly created by nature. Moreover, as a shaman's role is to cross boundaries, transgendered individuals were considered to be spiritually powerful and many perform religious roles to this day. Their power flows not from difference and marginality, but from their ability to incorporate the entire human condition within their form. They are neither male nor female, but neither are they a putative third gender. Rather, they flow fluidly among all three.

In shamanic communities, transgendered people are usually men taking on the attributes of a woman (the Chukchi of Siberia provide a rare example of the opposite[4]). This may be because many tribes, such as the Buryat (see page 56), believe the first shaman to have been female. Bronze Age rock art from Kangjiashimenzi in China's Tien Shan mountains shows larger-than-life females in ritual headdresses, while smaller males serve them[5]. Nordic shamanism was denied to men and Odin, upon gaining its wisdom, was said to have strayed into female territory[6]. Shamanism may have begun as a female tradition because women move more easily between sexual and gender roles than men. The dildos recovered with other sacred objects from Ice Age caves suggest women may even have ritually mimicked the male sexual role.

For the Yurok of northern California, menstruating women have special powers of healing and divination.

Newborn males emerge from women's bodies as if proving women spiritually complete, but men can only incorporate the female sex by blurring their identity. In ancient China any boy with shamanic potential became a girl, a *shih-niang*. In the 5th century BCE, Herodotus wrote of Scythian *enarees* (transvestite men in a sacred role)[7].

For the Iban of Borneo, the highest grade of shaman is a *manang bali* ("the transformed one"), a male who dons female dress and lives as a woman. While some only transform for rituals, such as the Korean *mudang* (see page 105), others live their entire lives as women. In southern Alaska, the *achnucek* of the Aluet and Kodiak people is a transformed shaman recognized during boyhood and brought up as a girl. For the Mapuche of southern Chile, shamans are either female or transgendered males living as women[8].

EXPLORING SEXUAL IDENTITY

You probably identify as male or female, but is this *all* you are? Try journeying to the spirit of your opposite sexual identity and ask for its help in understanding who you truly are. Every man has a feminine aspect and every woman has a masculine side. If you ignore that part of you born into another sex, you disregard a potent source of power. Learn from the spirit of your opposite sexual identity and make it part of who you are. If you have a helping spirit that is the opposite sex to you, try shapeshifting into its form. Does this experience affect how you view the world, providing another source of wisdom to exploit?

In Lakota tradition, transgendered *anukite ihanblapi* complete the sacred transformation through sexual relations and marriage with heterosexual men, sanctioned by the community. Transgendered Mahu shamans from Hawaii are also receptive partners to men. Alaskan *achnucek* and Siberian Sakha people believe that transgendered shamans can give birth after such unions[9]. There are few traditional shamanic communities where transgendered shamans do not exist. We need to recognize that true power arises from blurring, crossing and ultimately unifying the two genders. Could you switch your gender for rituals or even for life? If the thought makes you uncomfortable, journey to the spirit of your discomfort and find out why. Recognize your body for what it is: a shell that represents but does not define you. Like the shamans in traditional communities, you can leave it behind whenever you want to, and change into something else. As we shall discover next, upon initiation many shamans are remade. Do not hold too tightly onto your own sexual identity, but remain fluid so that you may reveal the shamanic power that flows from your gender role.

DISMEMBERMENT

The spirits throw the initiate onto a black table and chop his body with their knives, casting the pieces into a large cauldron. When the flesh has boiled away, one of the spirits searches through the pot for an extra bone, one with a hole through it. Putting an eye to the hole, the spirit sees that the initiate will be a shaman. Now the spirits begin to remake the man so that he will be born anew, full of shamanic power.

SUBMISSION TO THE SPIRITS

Despite the terrible act of dismemberment, the individual does not die, but instead is remade anew. The initiate above, Kyzlasov from Khakassia in southern Siberia, related his story to a young Hungarian researcher in the 1950s[1]. The bone for which the spirts searched, known as *artykh syook*, was the sign that Kyzlasov was destined to be a shaman – his physical imperfection had already marked him out to the spirits.

For many shamans, their path begins with a terrifying ordeal in which the spirits rip apart their body, burning or boiling away the flesh, and sometimes even grinding the bones to dust[2]. As this happens only in the otherworld, there is no pain and the shaman's

▶ *Canoe of Fate* by American Roy de Forest (1974) depicts a shaman venturing into the otherworld, where a gruesome fate may await him.

130

132

soul is free to watch the destruction of the body. It is a harrowing experience of death, and the reason why many traditional people fear the call of the spirits.

When the spirits call an individual from the Xhosa people of South Africa, they usually appear in dreams as wild animals – often as lions, but sometimes as crocodiles or snakes[3]. They rip apart the dreamer limb by limb, devouring the body until there is nothing left. The Tantric Buddhist rite of *Chöd* (meaning "to sever") takes place to music played upon instruments of human bones, the spirits tearing apart the initiate's body with knives and flails[4]. Then demons and wild beasts rush in and gorge on the flesh and blood until nothing remains. Some initiatory journeys are less gruesome, such as the drowning or shooting experienced by the Inuit *angakkuq*, but the initiate still suffers death.

In Japan, the shamanic–Buddhist mountain hermits known as *yamabushi* are held face down over a plunging precipice while they confess their sins, returning cleansed from the ordeal[5]. Such close proximity to death reflects the shamanic tradition of dismemberment. In the interior of Borneo, the head of a Dyak initiate is split open by spirits and the individual receives a new mind with which they can understand the hidden forces of the world.

The surrender to the spirits is absolute. There are no half measures – the initiate must die. Although dismemberment occurs in the otherworld, it is still frightening and potentially dangerous for those who do not know what to expect[6]. You have been journeying to the spirits for some time now. Do you trust them enough to put your body in their hands and accept brutal dismemberment while a part of you stands by and observes what is happening? This is a test of faith in your spirit allies, and it takes a brave person to undergo the experience.

In some cases assaults on the physical body mirror what the spirits do to the body in the otherworld; they are a means of making the act real, a form of ritual theatre. In southern Chile, an experienced *machi* removes negative energy from a Mapuche initiate by violently sucking on her breast, belly and head with enough force to draw blood[7]. The following day, the *machi* cuts the initiate's fingers and lips with a knife of white quartz. Taman shamans from Borneo also find their fingers pierced during initiation by *baliens* wielding fishing hooks[8]. They embed these deep in the flesh to enable the initiate to feel and remove spirit intrusions from future patients. *Baliens* also pierce the outer eye tissue of initiates to enable them to see the spirits.

▶ **Ritual knife** used during the Tibetan *Chöd* ceremony of dismemberment.

REMADE WHOLE

In all cases of dismemberment, after the initiate is reduced to nothing, the spirits begin to build the body anew, sometimes adding supernatural powers. The eyes of a Dyak initiate may be rubbed with gold dust in order to see the spirits, and the fingers may be fitted with barbs to grab hold of wandering souls[9]. In Australia, to become a shaman, or "clever person", initiates undergo dismemberment and are remade with new organs replacing the old[10]. The spirits may use quartz crystals for the purpose, something that may be replicated in this reality: in eastern Australia, for example, quartz and pearl shell is inserted into an initiate's abdomen through a small incision, or else sung into them with sacred songs. For some initiates, even the replacement of organs may take place in this reality. We have also seen (page 60) how Igbo *dibīa* from Niger receive the eyes of a dog upon initiation.

Having faced death and annihilation, the shaman is given new life by the spirits. It is a frightening experience, but only a prelude to the risks shamans face every time they visit the otherworld (the dangers and trials of shamanism are explored on pages 134–7). On each journey the soul leaves this world for another and, in that sense, the individual experiences a form of death. But dismemberment is also a symbol of the great power of shamanism, bringing life out of death. It is an experience that will change your identity, allowing the spirits to remake you so that you may be born anew, full of shamanic power.

UNDERGOING DISMEMBERMENT

• •

Try this exercise if you feel ready to undergo symbolic death and rebirth. Alternatively, you may prefer to leave such an experience for a later time.

1. Journey to your power animal or other spirit guides and ask for their advice.

2. If they agree to initiate dismemberment for you, listen to and follow their instructions completely.

3. There is no set pattern for dismemberment, but your body will disappear in a violent and gruesome orgy of destruction.

4. Immediately afterwards, the spirits will remake you in a more perfect form. Trust in the spirits and be willing to surrender your physical body utterly to their care.

5. When the experience is over, return to this world and spend time integrating your new form.

133

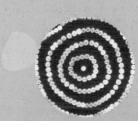

DARK SHAMANS

Terrified, the man waits. Kanaimà shamans warn their victim before they strike. At last they strip him naked, mutilating his mouth and anus so that he is unable to eat or digest food. The man slowly starves to death. The shamans bury the body and after three days drive a pole through the putrefying stomach. Tasting the sweetness on its end, they retrieve parts of the body to use in their practice, extracting power from a dark and evil deed.

134

TO HARM OR TO HEAL

The putrefying fluid (*maba*) of dead bodies allows the Kanaimà shamans of the Guyana Highlands to move freely through space and time[1]. They do not themselves undergo the suffering faced by many initiates, but instead inflict it upon a surrogate, the victim's life force becoming their spiritual nourishment.

In the Western world, shamanism is generally held to be positive, a view that does not always reflect the reality of traditional shamanism. "Clever people" in Australia have the ability to both heal and harm; in eastern Arnhem Land, in an endless conflict of curse and cure, *kalka* injure or kill by inserting negative energy into the bodies of their victims and *marrngitj* attempt to draw it out again[2].

Upon initiation, Shuar *payé* swallow magical darts that their teachers regurgitate for them. Sometimes a dart reappears in the mouth and the *payé* must choose between swallowing it and becoming a healer, or sending the dart into others to harm and kill[3]. The darts are pure energy, neither good nor bad in themselves. Among the Yokuts of California, dark shamans rely upon jimsonweed for power and may distort it to bring harm. To rid themselves of the dark presence, a community may call a shaman-killer (*hiautu*), who relies upon Hawk as a power animal[4]. The people accept that the *hiatu*'s power is used for good, even though it brings about the death of another

Whether shamanic power is good or bad depends upon the intention of the person who handles it. This is why it is so important to specify the intention of your journeys and your rituals. Reflect on the power you have raised on your shamanic path – did you see it as giving you the power to act or the power to dominate?

Similarly, it is up to you to decide what you seek from the spirits. The spirits are without morals because morals are relative and the spirits are absolute, so ethical repercussions are your responsibility. This may be why some dark spirits seem intent upon spreading illness and harm[5]. The !Kung hold evil spirits responsible for stealing souls and *n/um k"ausi* struggle constantly to protect people from them. For Taman people of Borneo, some spirits (*sai*) are petulant and potentially vicious, lodging objects in a person's body to cause illness. Mostly they act out of vengeance for a victim's transgressions, but they have few qualms about targeting the innocent as well. The *lwa* of Voudou tradition can also be petulant and punishing if they do not get their own way, and *houngans* and *mambos* take care when serving their spirits not to cause offence. *Wekufe* are malevolent forces encountered by the Mapuche people of Chile, and may manifest as an abnormal animal, a fireball or a blood-sucking ghost. While some act of their own volition, others fall under the control of dark shamans.

In Peru, individuals who feel envy or want vengeance will seek out a dark shaman (*brujo malero*), who either engages the help of a spirit animal to steal the victim's soul, or else fires magical darts into the victim to cause illness[6]. They work for their community and are therefore shamans, but of a type we might find objectionable. At initiation, spiritual practitioners among the Mississippi Choctaw must choose between a knife, poisonous plants or good medicine[7]. Those who choose the knife will be murderers, those who choose the poisonous plants will be sorcerers, and only those who take the good medicine will heal.

If you learn how to heal, you also learn how to harm. This uncomfortable truth is exploited by some. Even certain traditional rituals might make us feel uneasy, such as the sacrifice of a guinea pig (*cuy*) as a form of scapegoat during Andean healing rites (see page 159). Would you do the same? If you would not, does that make the people who do so morally wrong?

Are morals therefore relative, and if they are, how do you decide yours? Moral ambiguity reaches its height in southern Siberia, where dark Khakass shamans steal the souls of children, leaving them devoid of life force so they eventually die[8]. But they use these stolen souls to help their own patients recover from illness. Often communities with a sick child employ the services of another dark shaman to steal the child's soul back, inflicting harm on the person who now relies on it. Escalating soul theft often leads to prolonged conflict among dark shamans. But which ones act with positive intent and which with negative intent? All seek to heal, but in doing so they inflict harm on others. For Toba shamans of Argentina, power is a finite resource and they must battle other shamans for it, hurling rays of light at each other[9]. To heal more illness, the shaman must gain as much power as possible, yet this always leaves another shaman less able to heal.

Some of these issues may not apply within our Western world, but this does not absolve us from facing up to our responsibility for the power we wield. Shamanism challenges us to face up to its dark side and also to our own. You need to set your own moral compass, just as you set your intention before you journey, and decide what is right and what is wrong for you. It is up to you to decide whether there will ever be a circumstance in which you will extract power from a dark and evil deed.

GAINING PROTECTION

For some time, the shaman has battled the demon, rolling in the dust, breaking furniture and hurling his sword. He leaps up to the rafters to embolden the household spirits that cower there. Eventually, with the spirits' help, he prevails. To prevent further attack, he ties string around all present to bind their souls to their bodies and to stop the demon snatching them away. He also disguises their faces so the demon will not recognize them. Such precautions are necessary to protect against harm.

136

UNDER ATTACK

In Thailand and Laos, Hmong *txiv neeb* fight demons that invade houses and try to steal the souls of the inhabitants[1]. After the ferocious battle, the household spirits receive a sacrificed chicken or pig in reward for their valour. The *txiv neeb* then fortifies the house and people — adequate defences may avoid further attack.

Sometimes a shaman may be at risk. Similarly, there are also pitfalls to avoid as we go about everyday life. If you ever feel in need of protection, for a difficult meeting for example, journey to your power animal and ask for help. Your power animal will protect you and empower you with confidence to face your fear.

Inuit and Balinese shamans wear masks to face formidable spirits, the mask preventing the wearer from being recognized but also providing power[2]. To achieve similar effect, you can simply imagine pulling on the skin of your power animal (ask permission to do this first). This instantaneous form of shapeshifting sets up a barrier between you and whatever it is that you fear. To protect you further, couple this with the dance steps you formulated earlier (see page 115). Now look straight ahead and feel your power surge.

Spirits are amoral and so, while they may do harm, they have no specific intent to be malicious. Shamans from India believe that any spirit may become an ally if treated properly, so while shamans can and do defend themselves against attack, they prefer a gentler option of finding the cause of the spirit's distress. Breaking taboo — such as eating an animal that one works with — often angers the spirits. Minor infractions take on great importance until a shaman finds out what is wrong and seeks to remedy it — protection can be as straightforward as knowing the rules.

You might like to reinforce your defences by visiting your sacred site or by spending time at your altar at home. In Mongolia, people walk or ride around shrines three times in a sunwise direction to offer their respects to the spirits and receive their protection[3]. You can do the same, to connect to the world's flow of energy and absorb power from the web of life. Just as Thai people visit shrines to protective spirits before they start on the day's tasks, so you could pause every morning at a small shrine located close to your front door to gather power for the hours ahead.

You can also pause when you return, and ritually rid yourself of negativity. Certain Native American tribes have worry-baskets by the entrance to their homes, in which they place their troubles upon entering.

Uyghur healers (*baxši*) in northwestern China protect patients by passing ritual objects in a circle over their head (just as Mongolian people, to whom the Uyghur are related, circle a shrine). In Borneo, Murut shamans blow spells (*sasumpui*) over patients to protect them, while *kahuna* from Hawaii use chants to breathe *aloha* into another person, protecting the receiver by connecting him or her to the web of life[4].

In Java, shamans (*dukun*) speak mantras of protection or healing over a glass of water and then ask patients to drink the water, thereby absorbing the words. Sibe shamans (*iletu saman*) from Manchuria in China protect themselves by reciting secret spells handed down across generations, every morning for 100 days[5]. Words and symbols offer extra protection, and we shall explore these next. For now, journey to your spirit guides and find out how you can protect yourself, in your shamanic and everyday lives. Much of what you encounter will be safe, but such precautions are sometimes necessary to protect you against harm.

▶ **Inuit mask** from Alaska, representing the flight of a shaman's soul. Such masks are used by shamans to give them power during their battles with malign spirits.

137

SACRED SYMBOLS

The Navajo healer dribbles coloured sand through his fingers for hours, tirelessly building up a mandala on the *hogan*'s floor. When he is finished, others dance and pray around the image, calling on the spirits. Then the patient enters the *hogan* and walks through the eastern gate of the sand mandala to sit at its centre. The healing can now begin, the symbol providing a portal for the power of the otherworld.

ACCESSING POWER

Many Navajo ceremonies involve the creation of mandalas (circular, highly decorative and symmetrical ritual patterns) by a "singer" (*hataałi*) using pulverized coloured stone[1]. Designs often contain images of Yeibicheii or Holy People, who are called by the *hataałi* and enact healing via the portal of the mandala. The patient's illness is distilled into the sandpainting, which the *hataałi* destroys after use, safely depositing every grain of powder to the north of the *hogan*.

Tibetan monks also create sandpaintings (*dul-tson-kyil-khor*) to forge a link between this world and the other[2]. Many comprise mandalas with a wealth of important symbols. You might like to draw or paint your own mandala, or create one from coloured sand[3]. Work outward from a central focus, incorporating symbols that are significant to you and maintaining symmetry—for the Navajo,

a mandala's symmetry reflects the balance people seek in their lives. Then use the design as a portal to access the otherworld. Imagine entering a three-dimensional representation of the image, journeying through the various layers to its heart. Does this portal lead to new experiences in the otherworld? Journeying in this way could become part of your standard practice.

In Korea, at the start of a ritual, *mudang* draw symbols representing mythical birds onto paper, hanging them on bamboo poles outside the house to keep away malevolent spirits[4]. In West Africa, Muslim holy men (*marabouts*) make paper talismans, usually comprising text from the Koran or numbers of special significance, which they encase in leather, fabric or metal and give to patients for protection[5]. As Arabic (the language of the Koran) is also the language of their heaven, the words have divine power in themselves. In the Western world we tend to think of talismans, such as lucky coins, as bringing good fortune, but the *marabout*'s talismans aim to pre-empt harm. You might like to consider your own symbolic repertoire in the same way, dividing symbols that bring fortune from those that provide protection, so that you know what you need for any particular occasion.

▶ *Snake legend*, a mural by Hopi artist Fred Kabouti (1932), includes a crossed circle, one of the symbols that this Native American culture believes points the way to a better life.

MARKING THE BODY

The Huichol of Mexico believe that everyone is born with certain symbols (*nierika*) on their cheeks, wrists, throat and feet, but only *mara'akame* and the spirits can see them[6]. If a person falls ill, the *nierika* fade, so a *mara'akame* can diagnose illness and work to restore the vibrancy of the *nierika*. Elsewhere, people may inscribe designs onto the body through tattooing. Their own skin may have been the first canvas on which early humans worked. We have already met the Pazyryk chief tattooed with power animals (see page 62). In addition to the giant fish on his left leg, he had a griffin above his heart (perhaps the power animal he was closest to), a donkey, an antelope and tigers on his right arm, and a deer with bird-headed antler tines on the left[7]. Many of these animals are mythical, revealing the otherworldly origins of the chief's menagerie. You can easily use temporary transfers or special paints to decorate your body for ritual, perhaps with symbols of your shamanic practice or of your power animal.

◄ **Maori totem** from New Zealand, decorated with the sacred facial markings (*moto*) of this culture.

If you do not already have a symbol that is significant to you, journey to your power animal and ask for one, or set an intention to discover a symbol and then go for a walk to look for it. Holding the intention in your mind, remain open to whatever symbol might be revealed to you. Most of the symbols that we are familiar with, and that shamans use in their practice, originate in the natural world[9].

As well as recognizing *nierika*, Huichol *mara'akame* also use designs to bring strength to a person, creating beadwork images that hold energy until an individual is ready to receive it. These items become "power objects" – containers for power – and the next pages explore these in detail. Once again, the symbols provide a portal for the power of the otherworld.

SACRED SHAPES

Spirals and circles, such as the Neolithic rock art at Newgrange tomb in Ireland, seem to encapsulate the shamanic path – circles represent the unbroken cycle of life, for example, while spirals such as those at Newgrange may have been portals for spirits of the dead to journey to the afterlife[8]. After Christianity came to Ireland, people retained the sanctity of the circle; the Christian Celtic cross is enclosed by a circle. The circle-and-cross is also sacred to the Choctaw people of the Mississippi basin, and their shamans use it to invoke supernatural power. The Hopi people of the southwestern United States believe that their sacred symbols, which also include the crossed circle and the spiral, are hidden around the world and will lead those people who find them back to a life of balance and harmony with all things[10].

POWER OBJECTS

· ·

To mark the completion of her training, the apprentice *payé* stands before her teacher as he clasps his belly and retches loudly, gathering the power that lies within the phlegm in his stomach. The phlegm that he eventually regurgitates into his hand contains many magical objects and spirit helpers, although these are invisible to ordinary eyes. He hands the mucus to his apprentice and she swallows it, taking into her body the power of her teacher. From this object of power she can draw strength and energy and obtain help in her shamanic practice.

INNATE POWER

The Shipbo people of Amazonian Peru believe that a *payé*'s phlegm (*yachay*) contains the accumulated power of all the shamans who have held it and that, by passing it on from teacher to apprentice, its power will grow across generations[1]. Other examples of power objects held in the body are the crystals and new organs gifted by the spirits (see page 133), although these are personal and are never transferred to another shaman.

Power objects can also be held outside the body, such as those objects you already work with in your shamanic practice. A power object can be anything that holds and stores power. Some objects, usually those from the natural world, contain innate power and you may already have been drawn to collect such stones, feathers and plants. You already know that to access this power completely you need to journey to the spirit of the object and gain it as an ally. That way, you will know who to call upon when you need assistance, and the item becomes a valued partner in your practice. Inuit *angakkuq*, for example, work with animal parts, such as teeth, claws and bones, and believe that each is imbued with the spirit of the original animal.

EMPOWERING OBJECTS

Other objects, such as artificial items, need further empowerment before they can be used in shamanic work. *Angakkuq* might animate a wooden or ivory figurine by inviting a helping spirit to inhabit it[2]. By holding the figurine during rituals, the *angakkuq* keeps the spirit close and can easily call upon its help when needed.

You can do the same. Start by journeying to the spirit you want to work with and ask it what you should create to hold its essence. Make whatever item you have agreed upon and then journey again to the otherworld while holding the object and ask the spirit to move into it. The spirit might give you additional instructions at this stage, including a ritual for calling upon and releasing the power stored in the object.

Some artificial objects may already have a spirit lying latent and unrecognized within them. This is especially true of any sacred tools you might acquire that nobody has used for many years. While

142

you may be able to meet the object's spirit during a straightforward journey to the otherworld, there is also another technique you can use. Hold the object when you journey (or, if that is not possible, keep a clear image of it in your mind), so that it appears before you in the otherworld. Then travel back through time, watching the biography of your object unfold. Finally, see its creation, which is also the birth of its spirit. Get to know that spirit, then follow the biography of the object forward through time, staying aware of the spirit within the object and asking about its life. Eventually, see the object entwine with your life. You will find the object feels very different now that you have enlivened its spirit and gained another ally from the otherworld.

HOLDING POWER

An object and its accompanying spirit may provide help with all aspects of your shamanic practice, or the assistance might be restricted to specific tasks. Melanesian shamans use a crystal to diagnose a patient's illness, looking through it to see the spiritual cause of the ailment. Mayan *h'men* also use power objects (*sastun*) – often small, translucent stones – to diagnose illness[3]. The spirits guide the *h'men* to his or her *sastun* in dreams. In Tibet, lamas make *namkha*, crosses created from woven threads, which house beneficent deities (although others can also snare demons)[4]. *Namkha* offer protection to those who carry them, and large versions are placed above doors and windows to protect houses. These crosses also find a place on altars during séance rituals, usually accompanied by a mirror, another power object. The mirror becomes a temporary home for the deities, and by looking into the mirror the spirit medium will know when the spirits arrive.

Power objects can also hold intentions and aspirations for the future. The Hopi people of the southwestern United States, for example, use a prayer stick (*paho*) to embody a prayer for rain. You can do something similar by journeying with an object (perhaps one that you have made yourself) and passing your intention into it while you are in the otherworld. Keeping the object close is a way of

143

▶ **A Tinglit whale-tooth amulet,** from the northwestern United States, depicting a shaman on the back of his spirit animal.

drawing power to your intention, allowing it to manifest. Or you might like to leave the object on your altar or at your sacred site. The Hopi place *paavaho* (the plural of *paho*) at sacred sites around their villages.

SPECIAL CARE

It is important to look after a power object properly, and sometimes the routine can be demanding. Yuman *kusiyai* of northern Mexico treat power objects (usually crystals they call *wii'ipay*) as people with whom they have a personal relationship[5]. *Wii'ipay* require feeding, attention and affection, and may even get jealous of sexual partners – many *kusiyai* hide their *wii'ipay* when they have sex in order to avoid this problem! The *wii'ipay* imparts its demands to the *kusiyai* through dreams, but you might prefer to journey to the spirit of your power object to discover its particular requirements.

The Iban Dyak *manang* of Borneo keep their power objects in a box they call a *lupong*, and this

▲ **Nicobar Island *henta-koi*, a 19th-century charm that captures the power of the colonizing White Man in symbols of his dominance, such as mirrors, a clock and an umbrella.**

container absorbs power from all the stones, crystals, herbs and charms within it. Huichol *mara'akame* of Mexico store their power objects in a special woven basket called a *takwatsi*, while the *puyuma* of Taiwan receive a bag of power objects, usually collected by their teacher, at initiation. The teacher places the bag on the shoulder of the new *puyuma* as a way of transferring its power from one owner to another. The bag literally "makes" the *puyuma* and thereafter it rests at the *puyuma*'s shrine[6]. Their shrine is also where the Yaka *ngaanga ngoombu* of southwestern Congo keep a basket of power objects.

Whether you carry your power objects with you as amulets or talismans, or whether you keep them secure on your altar or in a shrine, pay attention to their needs and journey regularly to work with their spirits. As you already know, your shamanism rests on the trust you have for your helping spirits, so do not neglect them. Over time, these spirits will become valuable allies, residing in objects of power from which you can draw strength and energy and obtain help in your shamanic practice.

DIVINING YOUR PATH

High in the Himalayas, the shaman chants, spinning her drum and ringing her bell until her spirit helper enters her body. Then she turns to her patients. The first has a question regarding the outcome of a job interview. Placing some barleycorns on her drum, the shaman plays and watches how they jump and dance. By observing the signs and feeling the energy that they emanate, she lifts the veil of time and peers into the future.

SCIENCE OR MAGIC?

The word "divination" comes from the root "divine", suggesting the information obtained has otherworldly origins. This makes it relevant to shamans. Methods differ, but all divination seeks signs of the future through "divine" inspiration, which is then interpreted. Divination relies upon using the non-verbal, intuitive part of the brain to recognize symbolism, which is then analyzed by the brain's logical part. The practice therefore uses both hemispheres of the brain and is far from irrational. Some groups, such as the Azande of northeastern Congo and South Sudan, even attempt to verify its results with other methods. Thus divination is more akin to science than magic[1].

Just as the Ladakhi shaman above placed barleycorns on her drum for divination, so the Sámi of Lapland interpret how rings of iron and brass (or "frogs" as they call them) jump across the surface of their drums, which are often adorned with detailed designs of the four quarters of the world or the three realms of the otherworld[2]. You might want to use your drum in the same way, decorating it with a symbolic pattern in advance, or else intuiting meaning from the speed and direction of travel of the items you place on it.

Shamans use many other ways of foretelling the future[3]. Malay *bomoh* use a handful of popped rice when considering a patient's well-being, identifying the grains as representing earth, water, fire and air, and interpreting the combinations accordingly. Shamans (*wu*) from ancient China used "spatulamancy", interpreting the cracks and charring on the burned shoulder blades of sheep. *Puyuma* from Taiwan cast bamboo splinters, and Hmong *txiv neeb* from Thailand and Laos do the same with the split horns of water buffalo. In fact, casting sticks or splinters of bone is very common, and as far back as the early 2nd century CE, the Roman writer Tacitus recorded that tribes from Germany threw sticks to read the future; these may have been marked with a pre-runic script[4].

If you want to try casting with sticks, mark each one with a symbol and observe the different relationships that ensue when the sticks fall. Alternatively, gather a variety of small objects and cast these instead. The Zulu of southern Africa use four special bones they call *dingaka*, together with an assortment of shells, stones, seeds and any other objects that catch their eye[5]. To divine the future, the *sangoma* studies every aspect of how the bones and other objects fall, including their placement, distance from each other, and which side faces up. Igbo *dibīa* from Niger cast shells instead of bones and call on the help of the spirits for interpretation. You, too, can journey to your spirit helpers for their aid in interpreting the signs as the true power of any reading lies in the interpretation.

You can also wait for signs to come to you. Go outside and just observe what is around you — whatever seems important. A flock of birds may be pregnant with symbolism to one person and yet be entirely ordinary to another. If the meaning is not apparent, journey to your spirit guides and ask for help. Ancient Maya shamans (*nawal winak*) connected to sheet lightning for inspiration. They considered this a feminine force, containing all the mysteries of past and future[6]. At the ancient oracle at Delphi in Greece, a prophetess derived inspiration from the god Apollo, speaking in riddles that had to be interpreted.

The dead also hold knowledge of the future and there are many accounts of shamans meeting or even

◀ **Tsimshian shaman**, from British Columbia, Canada; the wooden carving is adorned with bear hide and claws.

raising the deceased to foretell the future. According to the ancient Norse poem *Voluspá*, the god Odin used his magic to raise a dead seeress, whom he questioned about the world. In Hong Kong, spirit mediums write down the words of the dead, dictated to them while they are in trance. The dead spirits guide the medium's hands and, in their own way, demonstrate power as only the educated can write[7].

Many shamans use mirrors to divine the future, looking for the signs reflected back at them. Indonesian shamans use crystals in this manner, as a lens that channels images of the future, and crystal-ball gazing is still part of occult folklore in the Western world.

Whatever signs you obtain through divination, and whatever your interpretation of them, remember that the future is not necessarily preordained. All you have obtained is knowledge of circumstances surrounding the future. How you react to these circumstances is as yet undetermined. The Zulu believe they can change anything they read in the bones, despite going to considerable lengths to obtain an accurate reading. Whenever you divine the future, always allow for the possibility that you can alter it by changing your actions. Set a new intention and work hard to effect the change. If the future looks grim regardless, then use shamanic techniques to protect yourself, and carry amulets to bring you better fortune, as traditional shamans would do. Always carefully observe the signs and feel the energy that they emanate, as you try to lift the veil of time and peer into the future.

DREAMING

• •

In his dreams, the shaman assumes the form of a bird and flies to the boundary of the village, keeping watch so that no malevolent spirits might enter and snatch away the souls of the unwary. The Highlands of Papua New Guinea abound with such spirits. If the shaman cannot defeat them in his dream state, he will return the following day in trance to fight again. For him, dreams and visions are as real as anything else in his world.

REALITY OF DREAMS

In the West, dreams are usually seen as metaphorical meanderings of the subconscious mind – they might reveal our anxieties and preoccupations but they do not represent reality. Moreover, many consider them a meaningless jumble of thoughts and images over which we have little control. Traditional people think very differently. The Ute of the southwestern United States dissect dreams to reveal the emotional motivations of the dreamer, and the Iroquois of northeastern North America do the same to uncover hidden desires, but both groups still treat dreams as another version of reality, not simply as a random flow of images from the unconscious mind[1]. For Mapuche *machi* from southern Chile, dreams are no different to shamanic visions and the word describing them, *peuma*, is the same. *Machi* believe that their souls

147

▼ **Zulu warriors** in Durban, South Africa; in this culture, a significant dream is acted out in order to share its message.

148

wander when they are dreaming at night, just as they do during shamanic trance[2].

How do you interpret the process of your own dreaming? Do your dreams feel more than merely images thrown up by your unconscious mind? Does a vivid dream seem more or less real with the passing of time than memories of things you did in this world? Dreams are an important aspect of shamanic work. Ojibwa people of northeastern North America consider dreams to reflect true reality, of which this world is a mere shadow.

For Baruya people from the highlands of Papua New Guinea, dreams take the soul to the otherworld, and whatever it experiences there is real[3]. Baruya shamans often supplement dreams with shamanic journeys, so they can re-enter the reality of the dream in a controlled manner. Injury or illness that occurs in dreams affects the soul, and in turn the physical body, which will require healing. This is also the case for the Taman people of Borneo. Dreams are the soul's journeys to the otherworld, during which omens may be received, and it is important for people to observe any rituals or taboos while they are there. If the soul transgresses, the effects are felt in the body.

SHAPING THE FUTURE

When Zulu people of southern Africa have a dream about the future that they consider important, they will often act it out to reinforce the message of the dream and share it with other members of the community. This makes the events of the dream more likely to come true. If the dream is unfavourable (and we know that the Zulu do not consider the future unchangeable), they will act out alternative scenarios to bring about a different fate. Acting out your dreams is a powerful way of identifying and reinforcing the messages that they bring and also of embodying any change that occurs at a soul level. If the dream presents an inauspicious portent of the future, use it to consider alternative paths and approaches. If an unfavourable future seems unavoidable, try acting out the scenario as you dreamed it, thereby making it come true in a controlled environment. Manifest the portent by acting it out and then move on. If you find acting difficult, then try doing it in the otherworld, enlisting your power animal to help.

You should always pay close attention to your dreams; we have seen throughout this book how important they are in gaining shamanic power. Igbo *dibïa* from Nigeria receive instruction from the spirits of their paternal ancestors during dreams, long after the individuals are dead. Dreams are particularly important for the Yuman *kusiyai* of northern Mexico, as the spirits reveal how they can manifest and develop latent abilities. In particular, the spirits guide *kusiyai* to the locations of crystals that they use to heal and, on occasions, harm[4]. The bonesetters of the Tz'utujiil Maya in Guatemala diagnose their patients' ailments with special bones, and they learn through dreams how to find and use them[5].

CONTROLLING YOUR DREAMS

Puha of the Great Basin in the United States sleep at sacred sites in order to meet their guardian spirits in dreams. You can do the same, sleeping at places that are sacred to you with the intention of meeting the local spirits through dreams. The technique of setting an intention for dreams is known as incubating a dream, and you can practise it with the exercise on this page.

We have seen that Toba shamans from Argentina fight for power with other shamans – the battles usually take place in dreams (see page 135)[6]. These shamans have the ability to take control of their dreams; they are conscious of being in the dream world and respond to events as if they were awake. Often, Toba shamans project their sleeping consciousness into the form of their spirit ally (*itagaiagawa*), which affords protection as they transverse the realm of dreams. Lucid dreaming in this manner is difficult, but it is possible. First, concentrate purposefully on incubating dreams and then set your intention to become conscious of having the dream while you are dreaming. If you do become aware of dreaming, you may find you immediately wake up – but persevere.

Many traditional shamans dream of the spirits or of their ancestors (who are discussed on pages 152–3) and this may be a good way of interacting with yours. By respecting the reality of dreams, you begin to release and harness their power. Over time your dreams – like your shamanic visions – will become as real as anything else in your world.

INCUBATING A DREAM

• •

To help with this exercise, you might want to keep a pen and paper or portable recording device by your bedside.

1. Start by trying to recall your dreams over several nights, writing down all that you remember on waking.

2. When you are regularly remembering your dreams, you can start to incubate dreams about specific issues. Decide what issue you want to dream about and set this as your intention before you fall asleep.

3. You may need to repeat your intention over several nights to make sure your subconscious mind has understood it. You are giving your soul instructions, just as you do before you journey to the otherworld.

4. Carry on recording your dreams. You should find that they now relate to the issue that you wanted to explore.

149

Traditional people know that the soul leaves the body while they are dreaming, and goes somewhere else. Dreams are not meaningless visions that reflect only the anxieties of the unconscious mind, but rather a version of reality, directly impacting upon the people's lives.

MEETING THE ANCESTORS

The shaman lays out the drum and power objects of her late teacher on the floor of her hut in the Nepalese mountains. She was sad to mark his death, but knows that the right preparations will allow her to hear his voice. Having created an effigy of his form, she waits until it is animated with a faint light. His spirit has returned. Death need not separate her from anyone she has loved.

CONTACTING THE DEAD

Many traditional people rely upon the help of their dead ancestors, sometimes preserving the bodies to watch over the community. When Angra elders die in Papua New Guinea, descendants dry out their bodies by smoking[1]. The mummies are then placed upright in cliff-face sanctuaries, to look down on the village and keep its inhabitants safe. During rituals, the mummies are retrieved to join the village festivities.

In ancient Egypt, bodies were preserved using advanced autopsy and mummification techniques[2], while across prehistoric Europe bodies were placed in peat bogs to inhibit decay. In Scotland, composite bundles of mummies were made with the head of one mummy, the body of another and the jawbone of a third[3] – the jawbone may have allowed them to speak.

You do not need physical remains to contact your ancestors, however, as you can meet them in the otherworld. As you journey, try holding a photograph or an heirloom relating to the ancestor you wish to meet. Then ask your power animal or other trusted guide to bring him or her to you. (It is best to limit such invitations to those with whom you have a connection, as spirits can decline them.) Huichol *mara'akame* may move the spirit of an ancestor into a rock crystal (*urukáme*), which remains on the domestic altar so the spirit can be present at family rituals[4]. The crystal is wrapped in cotton and tied to an arrow, reminiscent of those used in the hunting of Kauyumári (see page 84).

◄ **Mummified elders**, in the Asaro Caves of Papua New Guinea, continue to play a community role even after death.

152

The spirit is nourished with food, drink and the blood of sacrificed animals. In Hawaii, people make carved figures or masks to embody their dead ancestors at rituals, and the Nepalese shaman above did the same with her teacher, inviting his spirit to return via an effigy to continue to train her. By placing pictures of your ancestors, or some of their treasured possessions, on your altar, you invite them into your life.

By journeying to their spirits, you can make peace with anyone you were estranged from in life. Death changes individuals and even the most objectionable ancestor may have mellowed (this is not always the case, however, so use caution). Pomo people of California hold a four-day ghost dance in which they atone for their misdeeds. Those who do not make peace with the dead may become sick[5].

All members of a Huichol family share the same heart spirit (*iyari*), recognizing a lineage stretching into the future as well as the past. *Iyari* is a body of conscious and unconscious wisdom contained within the hearts of all members of the family[6]. In the Western world, we may have a different concept of *iyari*, possibly considering our ancestors to be bound to us through tradition or spiritual belief as well as blood. Your ancestors, whether through blood or not, have a vested interest in you and are one of your greatest sources of power in the otherworld. Journey to meet them, get to know them and make them part of your life.

HELP FOR THE DYING AND THE DEAD

Today, care for the dying is often delegated to health professionals. But your knowledge of shamanism may help elderly relatives let go of the body[7]. Even someone unreceptive to shamanism could try meditating with a mandala and may journey spontaneously. If the soul is familiar with leaving the body, it will find the transition easier when the time comes to die.

Huichol *mara'akame* also care for the dead, retrieving dead spirits so they can attend their own funerals[8]. Afterwards, if the spirit is not to live in a crystal, the *mara'akame* ensures that it flies to Wirikuta, home of all Huichol ancestors. In the Brazilian rainforest, Avá-Chiripá shamans (*nande'rú*) sing to the newly deceased to remind them of the route to the afterlife and persuade them to move on[9]. You may get the opportunity to sing a song of your own to the dying. And if you ever meet a dead spirit who has not made the transition to the afterlife – they usually inhabit the middleworld as sad and disturbed ghosts – call for the help of your power animal and guides, then explain where the spirit needs to go, singing your song as you watch the spirit depart to its place of rest.

Dead spirits may appear frightening and, as we shall see next, can even possess the living, but they are also a source of power. Your own ancestors are waiting for you; death need never separate you from anyone you have loved.

153

POSSESSION

The shaman beseeches his ancestors to give him power. The drums pound and the dancers circle, kicking up dust in the humid Nigerian night. The music steadily increases its tempo, until a dancer jerks uncontrollably. Now the shaman is at the dancer's side, asking which ancestor spirit has made the crossing. The dancer becomes quite still, embodying the form and power of the spirit from the otherworld.

EMBODYING SPIRIT

The shamans (*zimas*) of the Zarma people, who live along the Niger River, are rarely possessed themselves[1]. Instead, they oversee the dance and help alleviate the pain of possession. The possessed change into special costumes depicting the spirit, who takes control of the body and gives advice to participants. If the spirit gives specific instruction, the *zima* will make an amulet to channel its power after the ritual has ended.

In the Western world, possession is a staple of the horror genre, requiring intervention by an exorcist to free the victim. Yet in most traditional communities possession is a natural part of spiritual practice[2], a structured act that involves spirits with whom the possessed individual is familiar[3]. Like shapeshifting or dismemberment, it relies on trusting the spirits.

Possession is most apparent in agricultural groups, perhaps due to the debt of inherited livestock and land owed to the ancestors. Ashanti *akomfo* of Ghana are possessed by deceased ancestors at funerals (see page 123). In Japan, *itako* allow deceased ancestors to possess them in healing rites. In the divinatory ritual *ikikuchi* (meaning "from a dead person's mouth"), ancestors speak through the possessed medium (*miko*)[4].

In African religions of the New World, such as Santería, Candomblé and Voudou, adherents embody *orisha*, *orixá* or *lwa* (spirits of deities)[5]. Anyone can become possessed at the rituals, the spirit taking over their body, thoughts and actions. In most cases of possession, the individual welcomes the spirit's presence. Removal is only required where possession is unwelcome or the spirit becomes an unwanted appendage; Rajasthani shamans cast out malevolent spirits (usually a dead human spirit that has not made the transition to the afterlife) with protective rituals as unwanted possession may cauz zse illness[6].

Not all possessing spirits are ancestors. In Burma, the Thirty-Seven Royal Nats are powerful protective spirits that possess a medium (*natkadaw*) and give advice to the community[7]. People offer lavish presents, but can also inveigle the spirit to meet their demands. The *natkadaw* have to tolerate particular predilections of the spirits, such as a penchant for alcohol, tobacco or gambling. In Thailand, spirit mediums become the "riding horse" for spirits, which suggests an unequal relationship, but such spirits will obey a call from the medium[8]. Along the east African coast,

▲ **Baron Samedi**, the Voudou *lwa* of death, resurrection and sex, appears often in possessions and can be as entertaining as he is frightening[9]. In this painting, he smokes a cigar and drinks rum (at left, with "BS" on his hat) with other spirits.

a spirit "mounts" or "climbs" an individual[10.] Some are unwelcome, but others form a relationship with the possessed, who becomes the spirit's "chair", the spirit demanding food, clothing and sacrifices for its help.

You can try a gentle form of possession, embodying the spirit of an ancestor as you shapeshifted into your power animal (see page 71). If the spirit is agreeable, allow it to inhabit your body for a short time, feeling a human merge with you rather than an animal[11]. You will retain your consciousness, but new thoughts and emotions may come to you, and you may feel physically different. This technique is useful for obtaining a new perspective, and feeling the bodily strength of another within you can be empowering. You can also allow spirits to take over a part of your body, to gain specific abilities. For example, if you want to channel spirit writing, allow the spirit to possess your hands and nothing else. Always proceed with caution and ask your power animal to watch over you. Ask if you can do anything for the spirit in return. While it takes practice to feel entirely comfortable during possession, there is huge benefit to be gained from embodying the form and power of a spirit from the otherworld.

DIAGNOSIS

. . . .

Ancestor spirits burn in the body of the shaman as she diagnoses the cause of her patient's illness. For a time the burning within her would not stop; her Kazakh community said it was because she had turned from Islam, but when she accepted the spirits the burning ceased. Now, the pain comes as a diagnostic tool. She trusts the spirits and knows that with their help she will understand whatever is wrong.

CAUSES OF ILLNESS

Kazakh healers (*täwip*) are usually women (male *baqsɪ* specialize in ecstatic rituals). Ancestor spirits manifest as a burning presence in the body, and through this pain the *täwip* diagnoses and heals[1]. The ancestor spirits are devout Muslims, often Sufi, so the *täwip*'s commitment to healing is matched by a simultaneous commitment to renew her Islamic faith[2].

Illness is often attributed to an invading spirit; Shasta people of northwestern California believe it is caused by "pains", objects that lodge in the body and emit debilitating energy[3]. However, these pains are also a source of power. After dreaming of impending death, an individual called to shamanism falls into a faint and is approached by a spirit (*axeki*) with a bow, who shoots a pain into the person. This pain can then be thrown at someone else to cause illness or else be used to heal. By meeting more *axeki*, a healer collects many pains and grows in ability. Pains cause suffering,

but from this suffering the healer draws power. *Curanderas* and *curanderos* from Central America also believe that illness is the result of an invading spirit or essence that they need to remove. More attention is given to cause than effect: *ataque*, for example, is the emotional response to great shock and *bilis* is an overflowing of emotions[4]. Both lead to symptoms such as hyperventilation, diarrhoea or migraines, which are the conditions recognized in the West.

Many shamanic communities link illness to breaking taboo – the loss of energy allows a foreign spirit to invade. For an Inuit, eating fish and caribou meat together is a transgression that may cause illness[5]. Among the Maori, if a mother is having a hard labour, a diviner (*matakite*) discovers which taboo the woman has broken and may ask the child's father to remain in a river for the duration of the birth in atonement[6]. Toba shamans of Argentina believe that animal spirits punish breaches of taboo with sickness, and they negotiate hard to have the illness lifted.

Substitute the words "invading spirit" for "bacteria" or "germ" and our explanation of illness is not far removed from that of traditional shamanism. Indeed, Shuar people from Ecuador and Peru believe that illness is caused by either sorcery or microbes. However, Western doctors rarely seek out the underlying cause of illness, the *dis-ease* of the patient. Traditional healing requires the shaman or healer to establish why illness arose, and what changes the patient needs to make to be healthy. Merely withdrawing the offending spirit – the equivalent of a course of antibiotics – is not enough.

MAKING A DIAGNOSIS

When a person comes to you for shamanic help, first consult your power animal or other spirit guide. Gather as much information as you can about the patient and establish what you can do to help them (even if only refer them to a conventional doctor). Some people may not be ready to accept your help, and healing will also not cure the terminally ill. If a patient is going to die, he or she needs relief from pain and help in preparing for the transition – not healing. Atayal shamans (*phgup*) from Thailand journey to their ancestor spirits to ask the cause and nature of illness and, most importantly, whether they are able to cure it[7]. The *phgup* interprets the answer using a ball and board: if the board is moved and the ball remains on top, it signifies "yes"; if the ball falls, it signifies "no".

When you diagnose illness, you need to use all your senses: sight and smell, as well as touch, hearing and even taste. Huichol healers look for marks on a patient's body, and if these *nierika* are faint, they know that something is wrong (see page 141). Shipibo-Conibo *payé*, who live along the Ucayali River in Peru, use entheogens to see people's auras. These geometric lace-like designs are distorted by illness and also start to smell bad. The *payé* sing "fragrant" songs to heal the aura and restore health to the individual. Like the *payé*, use your shamanic intuition to see beyond this world and recognize non-physical signs of illness, too.

To establish where an invading spirit lodges, the Nähñu shamans of Mexico peer inside a patient's body using the image reflected in a crystal[8]. Tz'utujiil Maya bonesetters of Guatemala rub the bone they use for diagnosis along the patient's body and interpret the extent of injury from how it moves. Navajo "hand-tremblers" from the southwestern United States run their hands just above the patient's body; the trembling of their hands reveals the location of the ailment[9]. If you observe your patient while you are in trance, you, too, may be able to see into the body itself, whether you look through a crystal, use a divination tool or allow your helping spirit to possess your hands so that they move with supernatural power across your patient's body. You will be able to identify the invading spirit from its appearance: most Western shamans describe such a spirit revealing itself as something that looks entirely out of place, such as a lump of metal, a brick or a mass of tar. Extracting it is the next stage of healing (see pages 158–9). But for a successful diagnosis, just trust your helping spirits and know that with their help you will understand whatever is wrong.

EXTRACTING ILLNESS

The Tibetan shaman begins with prayers to the spirits, then enters trance. As her patient sits before her, the shaman drums to diagnose the problem and then suddenly lunges at the man with animal ferocity. Grabbing his skin between her teeth, the shaman sucks and pulls on the man's flesh. Finally, she gags violently and vomits a trail of blood and slime into a bowl of water. The shaman has removed the invading spirit and enabled her patient to heal.

SPIRIT INTRUSIONS

Lha-pas of Tibet extract illness using a variety of methods, all violent and dramatic[1]. Some allow animal spirits to possess them so that a wolf or wild dog tears at the patient's skin – and intimidates the spirit into submission. This is a technique adopted across central Asia, with Uyghur baxśi of northern China chasing patients with whips or touching them with weapons. Tajik shamans (*bakhshi*) from Tajikistan frighten spirits by stabbing a block of soap with needles, although they also appease them by smearing the blood of a sacrificed animal over their patient's flesh. Uzbek healers (*folbin* if a woman, as they usually are) actually whip their patients, and slash a knife just above the skin to cut away the spirit's hold[2]. This follows a diagnosis in which the *folbin* recites verses from the Koran and burps uncontrollably. The intensity and duration of burping give the diagnosis.

In Senegal, Lebou healers act out healing, dressed as hyenas (representing human weakness) and a lion. The lion drives off the hyenas, who take the illness away[3].

Like the Tibetan *lha-pas*, many other shamans suck out the offending spirit. These include Nähñu shamans of Mexico, who locate an intruding spirit through a crystal but may prescribe modern medicine once they have sucked it out and disposed of it. Ojibwa healers from northeastern North America suck the spirit into a hollow bone, then blow it into a bowl of water[4]. The surface of the water acts as a portal between the worlds, allowing the spirit to find its way home.

!Kung *n/um k"ausi* of the Kalahari lay hands on their patient and pull the illness into their own body[5]. As the healer is in trance and full of boiling energy the spirit cannot latch on, but it must be disposed of quickly. Shuar *payé* of Ecuador and Peru also take the invading spirit into their body, keeping it confined in the mouth, before returning it to the sorcerer who sent it or leaving it in the forest to dissipate naturally[6].

Piman *ma:kai* from southwestern United States and northern Mexico remove illness-causing objects, sent by sorcerers, from the ground outside a house[7]. This is a reminder that you should never heal your patient in isolation. To rid a house of spirit intrusions, you can use a technique similar to the one for clearing a space of stagnant energy (see page 10), then burn incense to bring back positive energy.

PROTECTING YOURSELF

When you try spirit extraction in the exercise on this page, call on your power animal so you are full of power and the illness does not lodge in your body[8]. Native healers in the United States may use a cupping horn, sucking to extract the illness, which remains in the horn. You may find your own tool to use in this way. You may also want to move the spirit into another object before disposing of it. Rai *jhākrī* of Nepal move illness into a banana sapling via a thread (see page 89), while healers of the Andes rub patients with a guinea pig (*cuy*) so that the illness jumps from person to animal before the unfortunate creature meets its demise and the illness with it. You can adapt this without using a living creature; Sámi *noaidi* of Lapland rub patients with a speckled stone, then drop it into a stream. When you have extracted the spirit, send it back to the otherworld, using water, flames or another portal. If you ever extract a human spirit, send it to the afterlife as you would for any wandering spirit (see page 153). Do not express any anger or aggression but accept that the spirit knew no better and that you are there to help.

Healing is one of the key roles of a traditional shaman. Modern medicine is effective, but may overlook the cause of illness — and here extraction can help. As we shall see, extraction will not work when soul loss has occurred, but in most other cases, removing the invading spirit will enable your patient to heal.

HELPING A PATIENT

Rather than sucking out an invading spirit, you may want to pull it out with your hands, keeping it safely away from the inside of your body.

1. Make your patient comfortable. Play your continuous drumming track with no callback (see page 6).

2. Without journeying to the otherworld, call to your power animal and perhaps shapeshift into its form, filling yourself completely with protective power.

3. Enter trance and examine your patient to find the location of the spirit intrusion.

4. Pull out the spirit using your hands or a tool such as a cupping horn or hollow bone. Make sure you have removed everything; come back if there is more than you can carry.

5. Pass the spirit back to the otherworld by placing it in water or using another portal that you have available.

6. Return to your usual state of consciousness and give your power animal your thanks.

7. Tell your patient that the healing is over and give him or her time to adjust.

SOUL RETRIEVAL

Spirits circle menacingly around her patient's soul as the Nepali Chepang shaman first lashes out to keep them at bay, then negotiates for the soul's return. The spirits demand blood and the shaman promises a goat upon her return. They agree and the shaman grasps the soul, returning rapidly to this world to blow it back into her patient. He will be a changed man, his misery and despair lifted by the retrieval of his soul.

RECOVING LOST SOULS

Shamans believe that a person has several souls, one of which can leave the body, with devastating effects. Soul loss is serious, causing lethargy, depression and even death. It is as prevalent in the modern world as it is in traditional societies, yet we have no method to counter it, only medication for the symptoms.

There are many causes of soul loss[1]. The !Kung believe that malevolent spirits of the dead steal the souls of the living and that *n/um k"ausi* must wrestle with the spirits to fetch the soul back. Asabano people from Papua New Guinea believe that a spirit may reach out and snatch the soul of an unwary person walking past a tree, stone or pool. The people of Cheju-do Island off the Korean coast believe nightmares are enough to cause a soul to leave, especially in young children. In the Western world (and elsewhere), trauma, through accident, illness or the pain of bereavement, can be too much to bear, causing the soul to leave. The soul might return of its own accord, but where suffering is profound, and when there is no intervention, it may never return. If it does not, the person will not recover.

If you feel, or your power animal tells you, that your patient requires soul retrieval, the exercise opposite explains what to do[2]. In northern Siberia, only

▼ **A soul-catcher**, like this Tinglit one from California, can be used to transport a soul during the retrieval process.

160

the most experienced Evenki *saman* would dare go in search of a lost soul. Many send spirit helpers in their stead and you, too, should rely on your power animal or other spirit helper for assistance. Consider working with others: in many communities shaman travel together in a spirit boat to find a lost soul[3].

When you find a soul, tell it that its owner wants it back (for this to be true, you may need to engage patients in their own healing, see below). If a spirit has taken the soul, offer it gifts to give it up. Taman *balien* of Borneo, for example, offer figurines (*sulekale*)[4].

Many shamans consider the family and wider community during a healing. In Japan, Okinawan *yuta* may find that an ancestral spirit has stolen the soul[5]. Ndembu *ayimbuki* of Zambia do not attempt healing until local social problems are resolved[6]. For successful soul retrieval, the patient's initial trauma also needs easing. In the Tibetan *bla-'khug* ritual, the patient searches for hidden objects representing the soul, thus engaging with the healing. In Malaysia, healing is enhanced by patients in trance acting out aspects of the subconscious[7]. After restoring their lost soul to them, try to interest your patients in journeying for themselves and in finding their own power animal.

Becoming a healer for your community is a hard and dangerous path, but it is worth it. After healing, a patient will be a changed person, all misery and despair lifted by the retrieval of the soul.

RETRIEVING A SOUL

• •

This exercise provides the steps for soul retrieval, but be guided by your power animal or other spirit guides.

1. Play your continuous drumming track with no callback (see page 6). Lie or sit next to your patient so that you are in physical contact with them at some point.

2. Journey to the upper- and/or lowerworld (the lost soul might be in either) and call for your power animal. Explain that you seek a lost soul and ask for help.

3. Follow your power animal until you find the lost soul. It may appear as a younger version of your patient or it may be in a different form entirely.

4. Tell the soul why you have come and that your patient wants it back. Gain its agreement. If a spirit has taken it, offer a gift in exchange. Gather the soul into your hands or place it in a soul-catcher (see illustration, opposite).

5. After checking with your power animal that there are no more soul parts to retrieve, return to this world.

6. Place your hands or your soul-catcher over your patient's heart and blow back the soul. Allow time for your patient to integrate the soul part. Later, encourage your patient to try journeying for him or herself.

EMPOWERING THE WORLD

· ·

The Kogi shaman's black hair blows in the wind as he faces the BBC film crew, high in the Sierra Nevada of Columbia. He chews on a quid of cocoa as he delivers his message for Younger Brother in slow, thoughtful speech. If Younger Brother does not change his ways, the shaman says, he will destroy the world. He must stop now. He has already taken so much.

A MESSAGE TO THE WORLD

The Kogi, an ancient people of the high mountains of Columbia, spoke to the world through a ground-breaking BBC documentary filmed in the late 1980s[1]. They share a traditional life, overseen by shamans (*mamas*), that seeks to maintain balance and harmony in the world. The Kogi, who call themselves "Elder Brother", believe the people of the Western world, who they call "Younger Brother", to be crude, uneducated in the spiritual imperative of Mother Earth and wantonly destroying the planet in a quest for material gain. The BBC documentary was a message from the *mamas* that was meant to make Younger Brother see sense, to educate us to care better for the Earth and its finite resources. Did anyone listen? Maybe a few – but Younger Brother continued as before.

Few now seriously question that Western lifestyles are doing irreparable damage to the Earth, depleting precious resources and even changing the climate, potentially leading to mass extinction of numerous plants and animal species[2]. The Kogi acknowledge modern scientific advances, but question the wisdom that leaves the Earth on the brink of catastrophe.

Can we do anything to help? Shamanism begins with personal empowerment, finding our place in the world and meeting animal and plant guides. We then look outward to our community, healing the sick and taking care of people as they progress through the stages of life. Now we need to look further still, and consider all humanity and our place on Earth.

For the Mapuche of southern Chile the world is a delicate balance of forces in perfect tension. Upsetting these forces, as we are doing through our unsustainable lifestyles, causes illness and suffering not just to people, but also to animals, plants and the Earth herself. The Kogi tell us that the Mother is suffering, seeing the Earth as a single being that sustains us all.

Rarámuri *owirúame* from Mexico seek balance among humans, animals, plants and the spiritual world through regular rituals[3]. Their word for "ritual", *omáwari*, stems from the word for "whole" (*omá*). You cannot remain insular in your shamanic practice. The power you raise originates from all things in this world and from all beings in the otherworld. It flows through the web of life, of which you are an integral part. We are all connected, all dependent upon everyone and everything else.

COMPASSION

What motivates you to care? You need to recall the suffering that brought you to shamanism in the first place – your period of spiritual initiation. Reach into it once more, plumbing the depths of your pain and shedding your own *lacrimae mundi*, the sacred tears of the world. Remember how your suffering made you feel, and how desperate you were for it to end. Then, and only for a moment, imagine that same suffering spreading outward to encompass your family, your friends, your community and, finally, the world. How does that make you feel? Is there a spark within you that inspires you to do all you can to cease the suffering of others? This is compassion: the overwhelming need to relieve others of suffering. Of all the power you have gathered and used on your shamanic path, your own compassion is by far the strongest.

The Dagara of Ghana believe that all people are born with a centre of harmony and balance that orientates them in this world and provides a means to connect with the otherworld. Through life, we lose our sense of this centre and are no longer able to tell who we are, where we come from, or what our purpose is in life. Shamanism puts that right. But we cannot completely restore our own centre until we restore the centre of all people, wherever they are in the world. Where one person suffers, so do we all. Is this an impossible task? Maybe, but our compassion drives us to try.

DREAMING THE FUTURE

The Shuar of Ecuador and Peru also gave a message to the world. They believe that we can change the world by dreaming a new existence into being[4]. They do not mean this figuratively: they say we can actually change the world through our intention. Mongolian shamans teach that heaven begins on Earth, within the hearts of each of us; all we need are the eyes to see it. What do you see when you look at the world and, more importantly, what do you want to see?

When shamans heal a patient, they may alleviate symptoms, but this is not their true purpose. By considering the patient holistically, including his or her lifestyle, environment and community, the shaman aims to remake the patient's world, to provide a new situation in which disease has lost its meaning. Shamans do not heal illness; they change reality so that the illness can no longer exist. This is what we need to do for the world.

The Kogi told us in the late 1980s that time is running out and the Mother is suffering. For the final journey of this book, go to her, meet the spirit of the Earth and ask her what you can do to serve. Draw on the deep well of compassion that is at the heart of who you are, and let the power flow. Dream the world how you want it to be. The Kogi are right. If we do not change our ways, we will destroy our world. We must stop now. We have already taken so much.

CONCLUSION

The woman groans at the pain in her side, but will not yield. To become a shaman is to leave behind the life she knows. She will not do it; the spirits must call another. Yet she knows she is only inviting more suffering, and in her dreams the spirits beckon her to them. Soon she will accept them into her life, following the path the spirits have laid before her.

THE CALL OF THE SPIRITS

In Russia, no Taman chooses to become a *balien* and the woman will fight her fate for as long as she can bear the suffering[1]. In fact, a Taman who did want to be a *balien* would be thought inauthentic and without power. Nobody goes to the spirits willingly. Yet Western people actively seek out spirits, and shamanic books and courses abound. Are we all inauthentic, without power? This is the charge that some level at us. But is this how you see your experiences so far?

The overwhelming factor in turning to shamanism is the spiritual lacuna in our everyday lives[2]. As a society we have lost touch with the sacred. Families fracture, communities break and even the planet is at risk. The spirits see this and they call to us: they implore us to take up the reins of shamanism and restore sanity to our crumbling world. Maybe this is why, in the Western world, the spirits welcome all those who heed their call, all those whose hearts overflow with compassion and the selfless desire to help.

Anyone can enter trance, but only by befriending and working with the spirits can one move from being a tourist in the otherworld to becoming a practitioner of shamanism. Becoming a shaman is harder still, as only a community can bestow the title and that only happens after years of dedication: healing the sick, helping the disenfranchised and walking a path of harmony, balance and beauty. Merely practising shamanism does not make anyone a shaman.

From the high Arctic to the Australian desert, people follow spiritual paths that we would describe as shamanism. There is no single tradition that can answer all our needs. What we require is a system that works for us and helps us cope with our own problems and issues. As you worked through this book, you have laid the foundations for such a tradition: your own. Have the courage to follow your own path, listening to the spirits and following their guidance. You need no guru, no books or courses to tell you what to do; just keep true to your own heart. Decide what is right and what is wrong according to what *you* believe.

Our world needs people like you. Ignore the critics and doubters. Look around you, just as you did when you began this book, and see how your reality has changed. Reach out and touch your power – it is a physical presence by your side. Now go and dream the world as you want it to be. Stretch your wings and fly, following the path the spirits have laid before you.

NOTES

Pages 6–7: 1. Kehoe 2000. 2. Hutton 2001: 29–44. 3. Williams 2010a: 32–6.

pp.10–12: 1. Simpkins and Alexander 1999. 2. Williams 2010a: 209–13. 3. Benjamin 1995. 4. Bruun 2008. 5. Collins 2004. 6. McNeley 1981. 7. Freidel, Schele and Parker 1995. 8. Silva Sinha, Sinha, Sampaio and Zinken (in press).

pp.13–15: 1. Lawlor 1992; David 2002: 13–110. 2. Allen, Davey and Friend 2006. 3. Endredy 2002. 4. Watkins 1998. 5. Stokstad 1978. 6. Myerhoff 1974. 7. Temple 1906. 8. Jacobsen 2012. 9. Tedlock 1992.

pp.18–20: 1. Taylor 2010; Carmichael, Hubert, Reeves and Schanche 1994. 2. Kensin-Lopsan 1993. 3. Myerhoff 1974. 4. Brown 2010. 5. Carr-Gomm 2011. 6. Tooker 1986; Pratt 2007: 533 (Morningstar).

pp.21–3: 1. Rattray 1988; Walter and Fridman 2004: 913 (initiation). 2. Jakobsen 1999: 45–146; Eliade 1964: 58–9 (stones). 3. Castaneda 2004. 4. Irwin 1994. 5. Fung 2000; Walter and Fridman 2004: 826 (vision quests). 6. Clottes and Lewis-Williams 1998. 7. Hedges 1985.

pp.24–7: 1. Eliade 1978: Chapter 8. 2. Anand, Chhina and Singh 1969. 3. Ball 2004. 4. Blacker 1975. 5. Wickler 2000: 198–222. 6. Bucko 1998. 7. Balázs 1996: 44 (Nenets); Williams 2010a: 178–181 (prehistory). 8. Reichstein 1999.

pp.28–9: 1. Sangarel 2000: 8–11; 2001. 2. Krupp 1997. 3. Berenholtz 1993. 4. Price 1994: 259–64. 5. Sun Bear and Wabun 2006. 6. Callahan 2010.

pp.30–33: 1. Harner 1990: 20–39; Williams 2010b: 9–23 2. Tart 1969. 3. Bourguignon 1973: 11. 4. Winkelman 1986: 178–82. 5. Anisimov 1963. 6. Blom and Sommer 2011. 7. Neihardt 2008. 8. Dorsey 1902. 9. Vitebsky 1995: 15–19. 11. Williams 2010b: 13–15; 48–9; 51. 10. Berman 2011.

pp.34–5: 1. Halifax 1982: 45. 2. Vitebsky 1995: 12–14. 3. Bogoras 1904–9; Halifax 1982: 9 (quote). 4. Perkins and Chumpi 2001; Pratt 2007: 319 (spirits). 5. Dentan 1968; Walter and Fridman 2004: 828 (land). 6. Jacobs and Kaslow 1991. 7. Pratt 2007: 308.

pp.36–7: 1. Magee 2002. 2. Holmberg 1992: 158. 3. Dreeden 1994. 4. Linn 1999. 5. Dow 1986. 6. Allen 1976; Walter and Fridman 2004: 777 (altars). 7. Mottin 1984; Walter and Fridman 2004: 809 (altars). 8. Turner 1967; Walter and Fridman 2004: 938. 9. Tambiah 1970.

pp.40–41: 1. Harrod 2000. 2. Medicine Crow 1992. 3. Courlander 1987. 4. Watanabe 1994: Takado 1994. 5. Winkelman 2002. 6. Joy 2011. 7. Heale 1995. 8. Glass 1988.

pp.44–7: 1. Zachrisson and Iregren 1974. 2. Rasmussen 1929: 55–6. 3. Katz 1982; Walter and Fridman 2004: 5; 894 (hunting). 4. Bloch 1992: 8–20. 5. Speck 1935; Walter and Fridman 2004: 10 (beavers). 6. Shirokogoroff 1935. 7. Balzer 1997; Czaplicka 1914; Walter and Fridman 2004: 620–2 (reciprocity). 8. Shirokogoroff 1935; Walter and Fridman 2004: 620–2.

pp.48–9: 1. Schaefer and Furst 1996; Walter and Fridman 2004: 401

(animals). 2. Childs 1997. 3. Bäckman and Hultkrantz 1985. 4. Bacigalupo 2007; Pratt 2007: 285 (animals). 5. Phillips 1965: 62–3. 6. Hamayon 1994. 7. Heale 1995. 8. Hadithi 1980.

pp.50–53: 1. Baldus 1974; Walter and Fridman 2004: 384 (ants). 2. Andrews 1996. 3. Clottes and Lewis-Williams 1998. 4. Miller 1983; Walter and Fridman 2004: 296 (antelopes). 5. David 2011. 6. Tick 2001: 220–8. 7. Miller and Taube 1993. 8. Zvelebil 1997. 9. Gayton 1930; Walter and Fridman 2004: 352 (weasels). 10. Sherman 2005. 11. Radin, Kerenyi and Jung 1987. 12. Sangarel 2000, 2001; Walter and Fridman 2004: 627 (hitching post).

pp.54–5: 1. Privratsky 2001; Baldick 2000; Walter and Fridman 2004: 580 (names). 2. Mutwa 2003. 3. Spevakovsky 1994. 4. Gayton 1930; Walter and Fridman 2004: 351 (totems). 5. Castaneda 1974: 118–270. 6. Dow 1986; Walter and Fridman 2004: 437 (rugi). 7. Steiger 1997.

pp.56–8: 1. Kaplan 1956. 2. Takado 1999: 89–93; Walter and Fridman 2004: 14. 3. Harner 1990: 57–68. 4. Williams 2010b: 28. 5. Tkacz, Zhambalov and Phipps 2002; Eliade 1964: 69 (origins). 6. Farmer 2009; Lüttichau 2009. 7. Diehl 2004: 123.

pp.59–61: 1. Barker 2006. 2. Williams 2010a: 100–1. 3. Mellaart 1967: 77–130. 4. Brunaux 1988. 5. Kindaichi 1949. 6. Umeh 1998; Walter and Fridman 2004: 926 (initiation). 7. Williams 2010a: 99–102. 8. Ashbee, Smith and Evans 1979; 207–300.

pp.62–3: 1. Walter and Fridman 2004: 15. 2. Rudenko 1970: 109; 112. 3. Fung 2000; Walter and Fridman 2004: 824 (animals). 4. Rudenko 1970: 253. 5. Ibid: 256–61. 6. Loewe and Shaughnessy 1999: 48. 7. Kruta 2004: 200–1. 8. Rosen 2010.

pp.64–5: 1. Blacker 1975: 140–63. 2. De Boeck and Devisch 1994. 3. Walter and Fridman 2004: 403. 4. Pratt 2007: 174. 5. Graham 1958; Walter and Fridman 2004: 727 (skull). 6. Hammond-Tooke 1989. 7. Dowson and Porr 2001. 8. Hamilton Cushing 1999.

pp.66–7: 1. Rasmussen 1938: 127. 2. Homer *The Iliad* 21.470. 3. Fischer-Hansen and Poulsen 2009: 23. 4. Walter and Fridman 2004: 621–2. 5. Jordan 2003: 101; 118–19. 6. Kaul 1995. 7. Pratt 2007: 12.

pp.68–71: 1. Valdez 1996. 2. Walter and Fridman 2004: 257. 3. Ereira 1990. 4. Williams 2010b: 39–40. 5. Wessing 1986. 6. Walter and Fridman 2004: 552. 7. Conneller 2004. 8. Bancroft Hunt 2003: 14–43. 9. Fenton 1987. 10. Slattum 1992.

pp.74–7: 1. Strassman 2001. 2. Davis 1997: 411–449. 3. Metzner 2006. 4. Jaya Bear 2000. 5. Luna 1992. 6. Pratt 2007: 439–40. 7. Vitebsky 1995: 100–2. 8. Ravalec, Mallendi and Paicheler 2007 9. Stafford 1993: 311–13. 10. Roe 1997: 133–48. 11. Heaven 2009. 12. Pratt 2007: 21–2. 13. Dunn 1973.

pp.78–9: 1. Schultes and Faffauf 1990; Walter and Fridman 2004: 386. 2. Walter and Fridman 2004: 14. 3. Castaneda 2004: 73–80. 4. Yasumoto 1996. 5. Cowan 1999.

pp.80–81: 1. Noll and Kun 2004; Walter and Fridman 2004: 87

(carving). 2. Fenton 1987. 3. Bloch 1995. 4. Graves 1955: 289. 5. Lucan *Pharsalia* 3.372–417. 6. Walter and Fridman 2004: 263–4. 7. Vorren 1995.

pp.84–5: 1. Pliny *Natural History* 16.24. 2. Ibid 24.103–4; 25.59. 3. Myerhoff 1974: 150–66. 4. Arvigo 1995. 5. Miller 2011. 6. Wright 2009. 7. Tick 2001: 51–2.

pp.86–7: 1. Illus 1992. 2. Walter and Fridman 2004: 828–9. 3. Kaminski and Katz 1994. 4. Hill 1992. 5. Elliott 1991. 6. Bach and Wheeler 1998. 7. Davidow 1999: 333–4.

pp.88–9: 1. Bacigalupo 2007: 76–7. 2. Umeh 1998; Walter and Fridman 2004: 927. 3. Arden 1999. 4. Walter and Fridman 2004: 329. 5. Wong 2009. 6. Allen 1976; Walter and Fridman 2004: 777–8 (healing).

pp.90–93: 1. Tyldesley 1998. 2. Plutarch *On Isis and Orisis* 80–82. 3. Neal 2003. 4. Herodotus *Histories* 4.73–4. 5. Hughes 2007. 6. Diószegi 1998; Walter and Fridman 2004: 594. 7. Alexander 2009.

pp.96–8: 1. Hultkrantz 1962. 2. Powers 1984. 3. Rappaport 1999. 4. Laderman 1991: 86–180. 5. Doshi 1989. 6. Clarke 2011.

pp.99–101: 1. Sered 1999. 2. Sangarel 2000: 17–20. 3. Biziou 2001.

pp.102–4: 1. Delgado and Male 2006: 62–4. 2. Williams 2010b: 60–4. 3. Kagan 1980. 4. Tambiah 1970. 5. Humphrey and Onon 1996: 147–52. 6. Sharer and Traxler 2006: 746. 7. Berrin 1978.

pp.105–7: 1. Tkacz, Zhambalov and Phipps 2002: 25–54. 2. Flaherty 1992: 73. 3. Pratt 2007: 255. 4. Walter and Fridman 2004: 599. 5. Yu and Guisso 1988; Haft 1992. 6. Nebesky-Wojkowitz 1975. 7. Eliade 1964: 146–7. 8. Riboli 1993. 9. Eliade 1964: 148–9. 10. Mottin 1984; Pratt 2007: 206 (costume).

pp.108–9: 1. Szomjas-Schiffert 1996. 2. Luna 1992. 3. Walter and Fridman 2004: 355. 4. Pratt 2007: 40. 5. Townsley 1993. 6. Walter and Fridman 2004: 385. 7. Ibid: 384. 8. Katz 1982: 122–7. 9. Kozak and Lopez 1999. 10. Perkins 1994: 130.

pp.110–11: 1. Murphy 1993; González-Wippler 2002. 2. Murrell 2010. 3. Williams 2010a: 149–53. 4. Arbachakov and Arbachakov 2008; Walter and Fridman 2004: 548 (drums). 5. Rouget 1985. 6. Pratt 2007: 282. 7. Lewis-Williams 2002: 224. 8. Conard, Malina and Münzel 2009. 9. Slifer 2007.

pp.112–15: 1. Katz 1982: 58–79. 2. Walter and Fridman 2004: 812. 3. Pratt 2007: 2–3. 4. Levi 1999. 5. Voeks 1997. 6. Evans 2011. 7. Roth 2002. 8. Martino 2005. 9. Rasmussen 1995. 10. Mails 1998. 11. Mooney 1991.

pp.116–17: 1. Walter and Fridman 2004: 700–1. 2. Ibid: 86–7. 3. Di Cosmo 1999. 4. Brandes 2007. 5. Speck 1995. 6. Kazunobu 1997. 7. Grimassi 2001. 8. Williams 2010b: 173–186.

pp.120–21: 1. Bloch 1992: 8–20. 2. Bonnemére 1998: 117–21. 3. Van Gennep 1960. 4. Pratt 2007: 29. 5. Ibid: 42–3. 6. Yu and Guisso 1988: 62–5.

pp.122–3: 1. Potter 1978. 2. Wright 1992: 158–165. 3. Bernstein 1997: 2. 4. Lewis 1989: 59–89. 5. Walter and Fridman 2004: 911. 6. Balzer 1996a: 305–6. 7. Reichel-Dolmatoff 1976.

pp.126–7: 1. Mutwa 2000: 70–2. 2. Asbjørn 1999. 3. Basilov 1997.

4. Isaacson 2009: 277–8. 5. Blacker 1975: 140–63. 6. Temple 1906. 7. Echerd 1991.

pp.128–9: 1. Nanda 1999: 21–3. 2. Roscoe 1998. 3. Fausto-Sterling 2000. 4. Bogoras 1904–9: 449–55. 5. Davis-Kimball 1998. 6. Solli 1999. 7. Herodotus Histories 4.67. 8. Walter and Fridman 2004: 259–63. 9. Balzer 1996b.

pp.130–33: 1. Diószegi 1960: 62–4. 2. Eliade 1964: 33–66. 3. Mlisa 2010. 4. Chaoul 2008. 5. Halifax 1982: 73. 6. Williams 2010b: 208–13. 7. Bacigalupo 2007: 82–4. 8. Bernstein 1997: 86–138. 9. Eliade 1964: 57–8. 10. Elkin 1994: 73–138.

pp.134–5: 1. Whitehead 2002. 2. Elkin 1994: 44–7. 3. Harner 1972. 4. Gayton 1948: 26. 5. Murdock 1980: 17–27. 6. Joralemon and Sharon 1993. 7. Carson 1999: 19–20. 8. Walter and Fridman 2004: 578. 9. Ibid: 463–4.

pp.136–7: 1. Conquergood 1989. 2. Mack 1994. 3. Sarangarel 2001: 137–8. 4. King 1990: 70. 5. Stary 1993: 230.

pp.138–41: 1. Newcomb and Reichard 1989. 2. Bryant 2002. 3. Fincher 2010. 4. Pratt 2007: 258–9. 5. Budge 1970. 6. Walter and Fridman 2004: 403. 7. Rudenko 1970: 110–13. 8. Williams 2010a: 112–4. 9. Macnab 2011. 10. Mails 2002.

pp.142–4: 1. Vitebsky 1995: 24. 2. Jacobsen 1999: 74–5. 3. Arvigo 1995. 4. Beer 1999: 323–5. 5. Levi 1978. 6. Walter and Fridman 2004: 882.

pp.145–6: 1. Evans-Pritchard 1937. 2. Eliade 1964: 175–6. 3. Winkelman and Peek 2004. 4. Tacitus *Germania* 10. 5. Ulufudu 1989. 6. Tedlock 1992: 53. 7. Potter 1978.

pp.147–9: 1. Thwaites 1896–1901, 39: 19–21. 2. Nakashima Degarrod 1996. 3. Godlier 1986: 115–7. 4. Levi 1978. 5. Paul and McMahon 2001. 6. Walter and Fridman 2004: 463–4.

pp.152–3: 1. Beckett 2010. 2. Pringle 2002. 3. Parker Pearson et al 2005. 4. Perrin 1996. 5. Pratt 2007: 547. 6. Schaefer and Furst 1996: 24–5. 7. Williams 2010b: 87–100. 8. Fernández 1996. 9. Pratt 2007: 39–40.

pp.154–5: 1. Stoller 1989. 2. Bourguignon 1973: 17–19. 3. Schmid and Huskinson 2010. 4. Blacker 1975: 152–61. 5. Murrell 2010. 6. Snodgrass 2002: 45–9. 7. Temple 1906. 8. Rhum 1994. 9. Brown 2001: 330–81. 10. Filan and Kaldera 2009. 11. Giles 1999.

pp.156–7: 1. Basilov 1995. 2. Lewis 1986: 98. 3. Bancroft Hunt 2003: 139–42. 4. Avila 2000: 43–69. 5. Eliade 1964: 289. 6. Walter and Fridman 2004: 871. 7. Ibid: 857. 8. Dow 1986. 9. Lyon 1998: 262.

pp.158–9: 1. Peters 1997. 2. Walter and Fridman 2004: 631; 644; 648. 3. Lock and Nguyen 2010: 292–5. 4. Pratt 2007: 540. 5. Katz 1982: 106–11. 6. Harner 1972: 152–65. 7. Kozak and Lopez 1999: 72–3. 8. Williams 2010b: 120–21.

pp.160–61: 1. Vitebsky 1995: 98–103; Ingerman 1991: 9–24. 2. Ingerman 1991; Williams 2010b: 137–8. 3. Dorsey 1902. 4. Bernstein 1997: 168. 5. Sered 1999: 25–44. 6. Turner 1968. 7. Laderman 1991: 87.

pp.162–3: 1. Ereira 1990. 2. Archer and Rahmstorf 2010. 3. Merrill 1988. 4. Perkins 1994.

p.164: 1. Bernstein 1993: 177–80. 2. Znamenski 2007.

BIBLIOGRAPHY

· ·

Books marked * are particularly recommended reading for building a shamanic practice.

*Alexander, J. 2009. *The Smudging and Blessings Book*. Sterling.
Allen, J., F. Davey and C. Friend. 2006. *Pilgrimage*. Ashmolean.
Allen, N. 1976. Shamanism among the Thulung Rai. In Hitchcock, J. and R. Jones (eds.), *Spirit Possession in the Nepal Himalayas*. Aris and Philips: 124–40.
Anand, B., G. Chhina and B. Singh. 1969. Some aspects of electroencephalographic studies in Yogis. In Tart, C. (ed.), *Altered States of Consciousness*. Wiley: 503–6.
*Andrews, T. 1996. *Animal-Speak*. Llewellyn.
Anisimov, A. 1963. Cosmological concepts of the peoples of the north. In Michael, H. (ed.), *Studies in Siberian Shamanism*. Arctic Institute: 157–229.
*Arbachakov, A. and L. Arbachakov. 2008. *Last of the Shor Shamans*. O Books.
Archer, D. and S. Rahmstorf. 2010. *The Climate Crisis*. Cambridge University.
*Arden, N. 1999. *African Spirits Speak*. Destiny.
*Arvigo, R. 1995. *Sastun*. HarperOne.
Asbjørn, A. 1999. Shamanism and the Image of the Teutonic Deity Óðinn. *Folklore* 10: 68–76.
Ashbee, P., I. Smith and J. Evans. 1979. Excavation of Three Long Barrows near Avebury, Wiltshire. *Proceedings of the Prehistoric Society* 45: 207–300.
*Avila, E. 2000. *Woman Who Glows in the Dark*. Thorsons.
Bach, E. and E. Wheeler. 1998. *The Bach Flower Remedies*. McGraw-Hill.
*Bacigalupo, A. 2007. *Shamans of the Foye Tree*. University of Texas.
*Bäckman, L. and Å. Hultkrantz (eds.) 1985. *Saami Pre-Christian Religion*. Almqvist and Wiksell.
Balázs, J. 1996. The Hungarian shaman's technique of trance induction. In Diószegi, V. and M. Hoppál (eds.), *Folk Beliefs and Shamanic Traditions in Siberia*. Akadémiai Kiadó: 26–48.
*Baldick, J. 2000. *Animal and Shaman*. New York University.
Baldus, H. 1974. Shamanism in the acculturation of a Tupi tribe of central Brazil. In Lyon, P. (ed.), *Native South Americans*. Little Brown: 385–90.
Ball, P. 2004. *The Elements*. Oxford University.
Balzer, M. 1996a. Flights of the Sacred. *American Anthropologist* 98: 305–18.
– 1996b. Sacred genders in Siberia. In Ramet, S. (ed.), *Gender Reversals and Gender Cultures*. Routledge: 164–82.
*– (ed.) 1997. *Shamanic Worlds*. North Castle.
*Bancroft Hunt, N. 2003. *Shamanism in North America*. Firefly.
Barker, G. 2006. *The Agricultural Revolution in Prehistory*. Oxford University.
Basilov, V. 1995. The "Shamanic Disease" in Uzbek Folk Beliefs. *Shaman* 3: 3–13.
– 1997. Chosen by the spirits. In Mandelstam M. (ed.), *Shamanic Worlds*. North Castle: 3–48.
Beckett, R. 2010. Mastering Mummy Science. *National Geographic* 218 (3): 140–2.
Beer, R. 1999. *The Encyclopaedia of Tibetan Symbols and Motifs*. Shambhala.
Benjamin, D. (ed.) 1995. *The Home*. Avebury.
Berenholtz, J. 1993. *Journey to the Four Directions*. Bear.
*Berman, M. 2011. *Shamanic Journeys, Shamanic Stories*. O Books.
Bernstein, J. 1993. The shaman's destiny. In Winzler, R. (ed.), *The Seen and the Unseen*. Borneo Research Council.
* 1997. *Spirits Captured in Stone*. Lynne Riener.
Berrin, K. 1978. *Art of the Huichol Indians*. Abrams.
*Biziou, B. 2001. *The Joys of Everyday Ritual*. St. Martin's Griffin.
*Blacker, C. 1975. *The Catalpa Bow*. George Allen and Unwin.
Bloch, M. 1992. *Prey into Hunter*. Cambridge University.
– 1995. People into places. In Hirsch, E. and M. O'Hanlon (eds.), *The Anthropology of Landscape*. Clarendon: 63–77.
Blom, J. and I. Sommer. 2011. *Hallucinations*. Springer.
Bogoras, W. 1904–9. *The Chuckchee*. Brill.
Bonnemère, P. 1998. Trees and people. In Rival, L. (ed.), *The Social Life of Trees*. Berg: 113–31.
Bourguignon, E. (ed.) 1973. *Religion, Altered States of Consciousness and Social Change*. Ohio University: 3–25.
Brandes, S. 2007. *Skulls to the Living, Bread to the Dead*. Wiley-Blackwell.
Breeden, S. 1994. *Uluru*. Simon and Schuster.
Brown, E. 2010. *Dowsing*. Hay House.
*Brown, K. 2001. *Mama Lola*. University of California.
Brunaux, J.-L. 1988. *The Celtic Gauls*. Seaby.
Bruun, O. 2008. *An Introduction to Feng Shui*. Cambridge University.
Bryant, B. 2002. *The Wheel of Time Sand Mandala*. Snow Lion.
Bucko, R. 1998. *The Lakota Ritual of the Sweat Lodge*. University of Nebraska.
Budge, W. 1970. *Amulets and Talismans*. Collier.
Callahan, K. 2010. *The Path of the Medicine Wheel*. Trafford.

Carmichael, D., J. Hubert, B. Reeves and A. Schanche (eds.) 1994. *Sacred Sites, Sacred Places*. Routledge.

Carr-Gomm, P. 2011. *Sacred Places*. Quercus.

Carson, J. 1999. *Searching for the Bright Path*. University of Nebraska.

Castaneda, C. 1974. *Tales of Power*. Simon and Schuster.

*– 2004. *The Teachings of Don Juan*. Arkana.

Chaoul, A. 2008. *Chöd Practice in the Bon Tradition*. Snow Lion.

Childs, C. 1997. *Crossing Paths*. Sasquatch.

*Clarke, J. 2011. *Creating Rituals*. Paulist.

*Clottes, J. and D. Lewis-Williams. 1998. *The Shamans of Prehistory*. Abrams.

Collins, Y. 2004. *Western Guide to Feng Shui*. Hay House.

Conard, N., M. Malina and S. Münzel. 2009. New Flutes Document the Earliest Musical Tradition in Southwestern Germany. *Nature* 460: 737–40.

Conneller, C. 2004. Becoming Deer. *Archaeological Dialogues* 11: 37–56.

*Conquergood, D. 1989. *I Am A Shaman*. University of Minnesota.

Courlander, C. 1987. *The Fourth World of the Hopis*. University of New Mexico.

*Cowan, E. 1999. *Plant Spirit Medicine*. Granite.

*Czaplicka, M. 1914. *Aboriginal Siberia*. Clarendon.

David, B. 2002. *Landscapes, Rock-Art and the Dreaming*. Leicester University.

David, C. 2011. *Find Your Spirit Animals*. Watkins.

Davidow, J. 1999. *Infusions of Healing*. Fireside.

*Davis, W. 1997. *One River*. Touchstone.

Davis-Kimball, J. 1998. The Kangjiashimenzi Petroglyphs in Xinjiang, Western China. *Indo-European Studies Bulletin* 7 (2).

De Boeck, F. and R. Devisch. 1994. Ndembu, Luunda and Yaka Divination Compared. *Journal of Religion in Africa* 24: 98–133.

*Delgado, J. and M. Male. 2006. *Andean Awakening*. Council Oak.

Dentan, R. 1968. *The Semai*. Holt, Rinehart and Winston.

Di Cosmo, N. 1999. Manchu shamanic ceremonies at the Qing court. In McDermott, J. (ed.), *State and Court Ritual in China*. Cambridge University.

Diehl, R. 2004. *The Olmecs*. Thames and Hudson.

*Diószegi, V. 1960. *Tracing Shamans in Siberia*. Anthropological Publications.

– 1998. Ethnogenic aspects of Darkhat shamanism. In Hoppál, M. (ed.), *Shamanism*. Akadémiai Kiadó: 83–106.

Dorsey, G. 1902. The Dwarmish Indian Spirit Boat and its Use. *Bulletin of the Free Museum of Science and Art* 3: 227–38.

Doshi, S. (ed.) 1989. *Dances of Manipur*. Marg.

Dow, J. 1986. *The Shaman's Touch*. University of Utah.

Dowson, T. and M. Porr. 2001. Special objects – special creatures. In Price, N. (ed.), *The Archaeology of Shamanism*. Routledge: 165–77.

Dunn, E. 1973. Russian Use of Amanita muscaria. *Current Anthropology* 14: 488–92.

Echerd, N. 1991. Gender relationships and religion. In Coles, C. and B. Mack (eds.), *Hausa Women in the Twentieth Century*. University of Wisconsin: 207–20.

*Eliade, M. 1964. *Shamanism*. Arkana.

– 1978. *The Forge and the Crucible*. University of Chicago.

*Elkin, A. 1994. *Aboriginal Men of High Degree*. Inner Traditions.

Elliott, B. 1991. Floral clock. In Goode, P., M. Lancaster, S. Jellicoe and G. Jellicoe (eds.), *The Oxford Companion to Gardens*. Oxford University.

Endredy, J. 2002. *Earth Walks for Body and Spirit*. Bear.

*Ereira, A. 1990. *The Heart of the World*. Jonathan Cape.

Evans, F. 2011. *Congo Square*. University of Louisiana.

Evans-Pritchard, E. 1937. *Witchcraft, Oracles and Magic Among the Azante*. Clarendon.

*Farmer, S. 2009. *Power Animals*. Hay House.

Fausto-Sterling, A. 2000. *Sexing the Body*. Basic.

Fenton, W. 1987. *False Faces of the Iroquois*. University of Oklahoma.

Fernández, M. 1996. Müüqui cuevixa. In Schaefer, S. and P. Furst (eds.), *People of the Peyote*. University of New Mexico: 377–88.

*Filan, K. and R. Kaldera. 2009. *Drawing Down the Spirits*. Destiny.

Fincher, S. 2010. *Creating Mandalas*. Godsfield.

Fischer-Hansen, T. and B. Poulsen. 2009. *From Artemis to Diana*. Tusculanum.

Flaherty, G. 1992. *Shamanism and the Eighteenth Century*. Princeton University.

Freidel, D., L. Schele and J. Parker. 1995. *Maya Cosmos*. William Morrow.

*Fung, J. 2000. Glimpses of Murat Shamanism. *Shaman* 8: 181–93.

Gayton, A. 1930. Yokuts-Mono Chiefs and Shamans. *University of California Publications in American Archaeology and Ethnology* 24: 361–420.

– 1948. Yokuts and Western Mono Ethnography. *University of California Anthropological Records* 10 (1–2): 1–302.

Giles, L. 1999. Spirit Possession and the symbolic construction of Swahili society. In Behrend, H. and U. Madison (eds.), *Spirit Possession, Modernity and Power in Africa*. James Currey: 142–64.

Glass, J. 1988. *The Animal Within Us*. Donington.

Godlier, M. 1986. *The Making of Great Men*. Cambridge University.

*González-Wippler, M. 2002. *Santería*. Llewellyn

Graham, D. 1958. *The Customs and Religions of the Qh'iang*. Smithsonian.

Graves, R. 1955. *Greek Myths*. Penguin.

Grimassi, R. 2001. *Beltane*. Llewellyn.

Hadithi, M. 1980. *Lazy Lion*. Little Brown.

Haft, N. 1992. Initiation into Ecstasy. *Shaman's Drum* 26: 36–45.

*Halifax, J. 1982. *Shaman*. Thames and Hudson.
Hamayon, R. 1994. Shamanism. In Irimoto, T. and T. Yamada (eds.), *Circumpolar Religion and Ecology*. University of Tokyo: 109–23.
Hamilton Cushing, F. 1999. *Zuni Fetishes*. K. C.
Hammond-Tooke, W. 1989. *Rituals and Medicines*. Ad Donker.
*Harner, M. 1972. *The Jívaro*. University of California.
*– 1990. *The Way of the Shaman*. Harper and Row.
Harrod, H. 2000. *The Animals Came Dancing*. University of Arizona.
Heale, J. 1995. *True African Animal Tales*. Stuik.
Heaven, R. 2009. *The Hummingbird's Journey to God*. O Books.
Hedges, K. 1985. Rock art portrayals of shamanic transformation and magical fight. In Hedges, K. (ed.), *Rock Art Papers: Volume 2*. San Diego Museum of Man: 83–94.
Hill, J. 1992. The Flower World of Old Uto-Aztecan. *Journal of Anthropological Research* 48: 117–44.
Holmberg, D. 1992. *Order in Paradox*. Cornell University.
*Hughes, K. 2007. *The Incense Bible*. Routledge.
Hultkrantz, A. 1962. Spirit lodge. In Edsman, C.-M. (ed.), *Studies in Shamanism*. Almqvist and Wiksell: 32–68.
Humphrey, C. and U. Onon. 1996. *Shamans and Elders*. Oxford University.
*Hutton, R. 2001. *Shamans*. Hambledon and London.
Illus, B. 1992. The concept of nihue among the Shipibo-Conibo of eastern Peru. In Langdon, E., J. Matteson and G. Baer (eds.), *Portals of Power*. University of New Mexico: 63–77.
*Ingerman, S. 1991. *Soul Retrieval*. Harper Collins.
Irwin, L. 1994. *The Dream Seekers*. University of Oklahoma.
Isaacson, R. 2009. *The Horse Boy*. Viking.
Jacobs, C. and A. Kaslow. 1991. *The Spiritual Churches of New Orleans*. University of Tennessee.
Jacobsen, K. 2012. *Pilgrimage in the Hindu Tradition*. Routledge.
*Jakobsen, M. 1999. *Shamanism*. Berghahn.
*Jaya Bear. 2000. *Amazon Magic*. Colibri.
*Joralemon, D. and D. Sharon. 1993. *Sorcery and Shamanism*. University of Utah.
*Jordan, P. 2003. *Material Culture and Sacred Landscape*. Altamira.
Joy, M. 2011. *Why We Love Dogs, Eat Pigs and Wear Cows*. Weiser.
*Kagan, R. (ed) 1980. The Chinese Approach to Shamanism. *Chinese Sociology and Anthropology* 12: 3–135.
Kaminski, P. and R. Katz. 1994. *Flower Essence Repertory*. Flower Essence Society.
Kaplan, L. 1956. Tonal and Nagual in Coastal Oaxaca. *Journal of American Folklore* 69: 363–8.
*Katz, R. 1982. *Boiling Energy*. Harvard University.
Kaul, F. 1995. The Gundestrup Cauldron Reconsidered. *Acta Archaeologica* 66: 1–38.

Kazunobu, I. 1997. Bear rituals of the Matagi and the Ainu in northern Japan. In Takashi, I. and Y. Takado (eds.), *Circumpolar Animism and Shamanism*. Hokkaido University: 55–63
Kehoe, A. 2000. *Shamans and Religion*. Waveland.
Kensin-Lopsan, M. 1993. *Magic of Tuvan Shamans*. Novosty Tuva.
Kindaichi, K. 1949. The Concepts behind the Ainu Bear Festival (Kumamatsuri). *Southwestern Journal of Anthropology*: 345–50.
King, S. 1990. *Urban Shaman*. Touchstone.
Kozak, D. and D. Lopez. 1999. *Devil Sickness, Devil Songs*. Smithsonian.
Krupp, E. 1997. *Skywatchers, Shamans and Kings*. John Wiley.
Kruta, V. 2004. *Celts*. Chêne-Hachette.
Laderman, C. 1991. *Taming the Wind of Desire*. University of California.
Lawlor, R. 1992. *Voices of the First Day*. Inner Traditions.
Levi, J. 1978. Wii'ipay. *The Journal of Californian Anthropology* 5: 42–52.
– 1999. The Embodiment of a Working Identity: Power and Process in Rarámuri Ritual Healing. *American Indian Culture and Research Journal* 23: 13–46.
Lewis, I. 1986. *Religion in Context*. Cambridge University.
*– 1989. *Ecstatic Religion*. Routledge.
Lewis-Williams, D. 2002. *The Mind in the Cave*. Thames and Hudson.
Linn, D. 1999. *Altars*. Rider.
Lock, M. and V.-K. Nguyen. 2010. *An Anthropology of Biomedicine*. Wiley-Blackwell.
Loewe, M. and E. Shaughnessy. 1999. *The Cambridge History of Ancient China*. Cambridge University.
*Luna, L. 1992. Icaros. In Langdon, E., J. Matteson and G. Baer (eds.), *Portals of Power*. University of New Mexico: 231–53.
Lüttichau, C. 2009. *Animal Spirit Guides*. Cico.
Lyon, W. 1998. *Encyclopaedia of Native American Healing*. Norton.
Mack, J. (ed.) 1994. *Masks*. British Museum.
Macnab, M. 2011. *Design by Nature*. New Riders.
Magee, M. 2002. *Peruvian Shamanism*. Heart of the Healer.
Mails, T. 1998 *Sundancing*. Council Oak.
– 2002. *The Hopi Survival Kit*. Penguin.
Martino, E. de. 2005. *The Land of Remorse*. Free Association.
McNeley, J. 1981. *Holy Wind in Navajo Philosophy*. University of Arizona.
Medicine Crow, J. 1992. *From the Heart of the Crow Country*. Orion.
Mellaart, J. 1967. *Çatal Hüyük*. Thames and Hudson.
Merrill, W. 1988. *Rarámuri Souls*. Smithsonian.
*Metzner, R. (ed.) 2006. *Sacred Vine of Spirits*. Park Street.
Miller, J. 1983. Basin Religion and Theology. *Journal of California and Great Basin Anthropology* 5: 66–86.

169

Miller, M. 2011. *Shamanic Gardening*. Process.
– and K. Taube. 1993. *The Gods and Symbols of Ancient Mexico and the Maya*. Thames and Hudson.
Mlisa, N. 2010. *Ukuthwasa*. Lambert.
Mooney, J. 1991. *The Ghost-Dance Religion and Wounded Knee*. Dover.
Mottin, J. 1984. *A Hmong Shaman's Séance*. Asian Folklore Studies 43: 99–108.
Murdock, G. 1980. *Theories of Illness*. University of Pittsburgh.
Murphy, J. 1993. Santería. Beacon.
*Murrell, N. 2010. *Afro-Caribbean Religions*. Temple University.
Mutwa, V. 2000. *The Song of Stars*. Barrytown.
*– 2003. *Zulu Shaman*. Destiny.
Myerhoff, B. 1974. *Peyote Hunt*. Cornell University.
Nakashima Degarrod, L. 1996. Mapuche. In Levinson, D. (ed.), *Portraits of Culture*. Prentice-Hall: 237–64.
Nanda, S. 1999. *Gender Diversity*. Waveland.
Neal, C. 2003. *Incense*. Llewellyn.
Nebesky-Wojkowitz, R. de. 1975. *Oracles and Demons of Tibet*. Druck-Verlagsanstalt.
*Neihardt, J. 2008. *Black Elk Speaks*. University of New York.
Newcomb, F. and G. Reichard. 1989. *Sandpaintings of the Navajo Shooting Chant*. Dover.
Noll, R. and S. Kun. 2004. Chuonnasuan. *Journal of Korean Religions* 6: 135-162.
Parker Pearson, M., A. Chamberlain, O. Craig et al. 2005. Evidence for Mummification in Bronze Age Britain. *Antiquity* 79: 529–46.
Paul, B. and C. McMahon. 2001. Mesoamerican bonesetters. In Huber, B. and A. Sandstrom (eds.), *Mesoamerican Healers*. University of Texas: 243–69.
*Perkins, J. 1994. *The World Is As You Dream It*. Destiny.
– and S. Chumpi. 2001. *Spirit of the Shuar*. Destiny.
Perrin, M. 1996. The urukáme. A crystallization of the soul. In Schaefer, S. and P. Furst (eds.), *People of the Peyote*. University of New Mexico: 403–28.
Peters, L. 1997. The Tibetan Healing Rituals of Dorje Yüdronma. *Shaman's Drum* 45: 36–47.
Phillips, E. 1965. *The Royal Hordes*. Thames and Hudson.
Potter, J. 1978. Cantonese shamanism. In Wolf, A. (ed.), *Studies in Chinese Society*. Stanford University: 321–46.
Powers, W. 1984. *Yuwipi*. University of Nebraska.
*Pratt, C. 2007. *An Encyclopaedia of Shamanism*. Rosen.
Price, N. 1994. Tourism and the Bighorn medicine wheel. In Carmichael, D., J. Hubert, B. Reeves and A. Schanche (eds.), *Sacred Sites, Sacred Places*. Routledge: 259–64.
Pringle, H. 2002. *The Mummy Congress*. Fourth Estate.
Privratsky, B. 2001. *Muslim Turkistan*. Curzon.

Radin, P., C. Kerenyi and C. Jung. 1987. *Trickster*. Schocken.
Rappaport, R. 1999. *Ritual and Religion in the Making of Humanity*. Cambridge University.
Rasmussen, K. 1929. *Intellectual Culture of the Iglulik Eskimos*. Gyldendalske Boghandel.
– 1938. *Knud Rasmussen's Posthumous Notes on the Life and Doings of the East Greenlanders in Olden Times*. Reitzels Forlag.
Rasmussen, S. 1995. *Spirit Possession and Personhood Among the Kel Ewey Tuareg*. Cambridge University.
Rattray, R. 1988. *Religion and Art in Ashanti*. AMS.
*Ravalec, V., Mallendi and A. Paicheler. 2007. *Iboga*. Park Street.
Reichel-Dolmatoff, G. 1976. Training for the priesthood among the Kogi of Columbia. In Wilbert, J. (ed.), *Enculturation in Latin America*. University of California: 265–88.
Reichstein, G. 1999. *Wood Becomes Water*. Kodansha America.
*Rhum, M. 1994. *The Ancestral Lords*. Northern Illinois University.
Riboli, D. 1993. Shamanic paraphernalia and dances among the Chepang shamans. In Hoppál, M. and T. Kim (eds.), *Shamanism and Performing Arts*. Hungarian Academy of Sciences: 122–7.
Roe, P. 1997. Just wasting away. In Bercht, F., E. Brodsky, J.Farmer and D. Taylor (eds), *Taíno*. Monacelli.
Roscoe, W. 1998. *Changing Ones*. University of New Mexico.
Rosen, B. 2010. *The Mythical Creatures Bible*. Godsfield.
*Roth, G. 2002. *Sweat Your Prayers*. Tarcher.
Rouget, G. 1985. *Music and Trance*. Chicago University.
Rudenko, S. 1970. *Frozen Tombs of Siberia*. Dent.
*Sangarel. 2000. *Riding Windhorses*. Destiny.
– 2001. *Chosen by the Spirits*. Destiny.
*Schaefer, S. and P. Furst (eds.) 1996. *People of the Peyote*. University of New Mexico.
*Schmid, B. and L. Huskinson. 2010. *Spirit Possession and Trance*. Continuum.
Schultes, R. and R. Raffauf. 1990. *The Healing Forest*. Dioscorides.
Sered, S. 1999. *Women of the Sacred Groves*. Oxford University.
Sharer, R. and L. Traxler. 2006. *The Ancient Maya*. Stanford University.
Sherman, J. 2005. *Trickster Tales*. August House.
*Shirokogoroff, S. 1935. *The Psychomental Complex of the Tungus*. Kegan Paul.
Silva Sinha, V., C. Sinha, W. Sampaio and J. Zinken. In Press. Event-based time intervals in an Amazonian culture. In Filipović, L. and K. Jaszczolt (eds.), *Space and Time Across Languages and Cultures II*. John Benjamins.
Simpkins, A. and C. Alexander. 1999. *Simple Taoism*. Tuttle.
Slattum, J. 1992. *Masks of Bali*. Chronicle.
Slifer, D. 2007. *Kokopelli*. Gibbs Smith.

Snodgrass, J. 2002. A Tale of Goddesses, Money and Other Terribly Wonderful Things. *American Ethnologist* 29: 602–36.

Solli, B. 1999. Odin the queer? In Gustafsson, A. and H. Karlsson (eds.), *Glyfer och Arkeologiska Rum*. Gotarc: 341–9.

Speck, F. 1935. *Naskapi*. University of Oklahoma.

– 1995. *Midwinter Rites of the Cayuga Long House*. University of Nebraska.

Spevakovsky, A. 1994. Animal cults and ecology. In Takashi, I. and Y. Takado (eds.), *Circumpolar Religion and Ecology*. University of Tokyo: 103–9.

Stafford, P. 1993. *Psychedelics Encyclopaedia*. Ronin.

Stary, G. 1993. The "secret handbook" of a Sibe shaman. In Hoppál, M. and K. Howard (eds.), *Shamans and Cultures*. Society for Trans-Oceanic Research: 229–39.

Steiger, B. 1997. *Totems*. Harper Collins.

Stokstad, M. 1978. *Santiago de Compostela in the Age of the Great Pilgrimages*. University of Oklahoma.

Stoller, P. 1989. *Fusion of the Worlds*. University of Chicago.

*Strassman, R. 2001. *DMT*. Inner Traditions.

*Sun Bear and Wabun. 2006. *The Medicine Wheel*. Simon and Schuster.

Szomjas-Schiffert, G. 1996. *Singing Tradition of Lapp Shamans*. Akadémiai Kiadó.

Takado, Y. 1994. Animals as the intersection of religion and ecology. In Takashi, I. and Y. Takado (eds.), *Circumpolar Religion and Ecology*. University of Tokyo: 69–103.

*– 1999. *An Anthropology of Animism and Shamanism*. Akadémiai Kiadó.

Tambiah, S. 1970. *Buddhism and the Spirit Cults of North-East Thailand*. Cambridge University.

*Tart, C. (ed.) 1969. *Altered States of Consciousness*. Wiley.

Taylor, A. 2010. *The Sacred Sites Bible*. Godsfield.

Tedlock, B. 1992. *Time and the Highland Maya*. University of New Mexico.

Temple, R. 1906. *The Thirty-Seven Nats*. Griggs.

Thwaites, R. (ed.) 1896–1901. *The Jesuit Relations and Allied Documents*. Burrows.

*Tick, E. 2001. *The Practice of Dream Healing*. Quest.

*Tkacz, V., S. Zhambalov and W. Phipps. 2002. *Shanar*. Parabola.

Tooker, E. 1986. *An Iroquois Source Book 3: Medicine Society Rituals*. Garland.

Townsley, G. 1993. Song Paths. *L'Homme* 33: 449–68.

Turner, V. 1967. *The Forest of Symbols*. Cornell University.

– 1968. *The Drums of Affliction*. Clarendon.

Tyldesley, J. 1998. *Hatchepsut*. Penguin.

Ulufudu. 1989. *Zulu Bone Oracle*. Wingbow.

*Umeh, J. 1998. *After God is Dibia*. Karnak House.

Valdez, S. 1996. Wolf power and interspecies communication in Huichol shamanism. In Schaefer, S. and P. Furst (eds.), *People of the Peyote*. University of New Mexico: 267–305.

Van Gennep, A. 1960. *The Rites of Passage*. Routledge and Keegan Paul.

*Vitebsky, P. 2001. *The Shaman*. Duncan Baird.

Voeks, R. 1997. *Sacred Leaves of Candomblé*. University of Texas.

Vorren, Ø. 1985. Circular sacrificial sites and their function. In Bäckman, L. and Å. Hultkrantz (eds.), *Saami Pre-Christian Religion*. Almqvist and Wiksell: 69–81.

*Walter, M and E. Fridman. 2004. *Shamanism*. ABC Clio.

Watanabe, H. 1994. The animal cult of northern hunter-gatherers. In Takashi, I. and Y. Takado (eds.), *Circumpolar Religion and Ecology*. University of Tokyo: 47–69.

Watkins, A. 1998. *The Old Straight Track*. Abacus.

Wessing, R. 1986. *The Soul of Ambiguity*. Northern Illinois University.

*Whitehead, N. 2002. *Dark Shamans*. Duke University.

Wickler, K. 2000. Mami Water in African religion and spirituality. In Olupna, J. (ed.), *African Spirituality*. Crossroads: 198–222.

Williams, M. 2010a. *Prehistoric Belief*. History Press.

*– 2010b. *Follow the Shaman's Call*. Llewellyn.

Winkelman, M. 1986. Trance States. *Ethos* 14: 174–203.

– 2002. Shamanism and Cognitive Evolution. *Cambridge Archaeological Journal* 12: 71–101.

*– and P. Peek (eds.) 2004. *Divination and Healing*. University of Arizona.

Wong, J. 2009. *Grow Your Own Drugs*. Collins.

Wright, H. 2009. *Biodynamic Gardening*. Floris.

*Wright, P. 1992. Dream, shamanism, and power among the Toba of Formosa Province. In Langdon, E., J. Matteson and G. Baer (eds.), *Portals of Power*. University of New Mexico: 149–72.

Yasumoto, M. 1996. The psychotropic kieri in Huichol culture. In Schaefer, S. and P. Furst (eds.), *People of the Peyote*. University of New Mexico: 235–63.

*Yu, C. and R. Guisso (eds.) 1988. *Shamanism*. Asian Humanities.

Zachrisson, I. and E. Iregren. 1974. Lappish Bear Graves in North Sweden. *Early Norrland* 5.

*Znamenski, A. 2007. *The Beauty of the Primitive*. Oxford University.

Zvelebil, M. 1997. Hunter-Gatherer Ritual Landscapes. *Analecta Praehistorica Leidensia* 29: 33–50.

171

INDEX

Page numbers in *italics* refer to illustrations/captions

Aboriginals 13, 14, 24, 35, 80, 133
Ainu 59, 60, 64, 115
air 24, 26
Akawaio 108
alaska 70–1
Algonquian 20
altars 36–7
Amaringo, Pablo *30*
Amazonia 68, 78–9
Amondawa people 12
Amritsar: Golden Temple 18
amulets 65, *122*
ancestors:
    contacting 152–3
    dreaming of 149
    possession by 154
Andes 36
Angra 152
animal brethren 40–71
Animal People 40
animals:
    companion 55
    domesticated 59–61
    encountering 48–9
    hunting 44–7, 66
    kinship with 40
    learning from 42
    messages from 48
    names 40
    parts 64–5
    relationship with 41, 44–7
    reliance on 46–7
    respect for 40–1, 46–7
    rituals with 48
    rulers of 66–7
    sacrificing 59–60
    souls 47
    spirit helpers 50–3
    totems 54–5
    see also power animals
Ankave 120
Aparai 64

Argentina 122, 135, 149, 156
Asabano 160
Asclepius 52, 63, 85
Ashanti 21, 22, 80, 123, 154
    fertility icon *21*
Ashevak, Kenojuak *52*
Atayal 157
auras 157
Australia *see* Aboriginals
Avá-Chiripá 108, 153
ayahuasca 74, 76, 77, 86, 89
Azande 145

Bach, Edward 87
Bali 71, 136
Baruya 148
Batek 70
baths 86, 89
beauty 11
bedtime: ritual for 101
Beltane 117
Big Horn 29
Borneo 23, 35, 52, 86, 122, 129, 132, 137, 148
Brazil 108, 114, 153
Brown, Everald *112*
Buddhism 27, *90*, 107, 132
Bugu tribe 54
Bungle Bungle Ranges 16
Burma 15, 127
Buryat 28, 54, 56–7, 81, 105, 128
Bwiti religion 76

candles 37
Candomblé 114, 154
Carib 33
Castaneda, Carlos 21, 79, 85
Çatal Hüyük 59
cave and rock art 22, 23, 50, 77, 111, 128, 141
caves 26, 32
cedar 93
Celts 66–7
Cernunnos 67
Cheju-do Island 160
Chepang 107, 116, 127, 160

Chichén Itzá *103*
Chile 129, 162
China 102, 111, 112, 116, 117, 123, 129
Choctaw 135, 141
Chukchi 34, 128
circumcision 120
Coast Salish people 40
coca 76, 89
Columbia 68, 78, 123, 162
    costume *106*
coming of age 120–1
compassion 163
Congo 64, 76, 122, 144, 145
costume 105–7, *106*
Crow people 40
Cuba 110

Dagara 29, 57, 163
dance 112–15
dark shamans 134–5
datura 77, 79
Day of the Dead 116–17, *118–19*
de Forest, Roy *130*
demon: protection from 136–7
Desana 68
directions (cardinal) 28–9
disability 126–7
disfigurement 126–7
dismemberment 130–3
divination 64, 145–6
Dogon 111
domestication 59–61
dowsing 19
dragons 62–3, *63*
dreams 147–50
    of animals 53
    controlling 149
    of dead 122
    of future 163
    incubating 149
Dreamtime 13
Druids 28, 81, 84, 85, 116, 117
drumming 30, 32
drums 110–11, *111*
Dryads 82

Dyak 132, 133, 144
    amulet *122*
dying: care for 153

earth 24, 26
Ecuador 120–1, 156, 158, 163
Egypt 24, 90, 152
Ekootak, Victor *44*
elements 24–7
    directions and 28–9
    fifth 27
empowerment 162–3
entheogens 74–7, 78, 88
equinoxes 28
Evenki 47, 70, 105, 109

False Face Society 71, 80
feathers 64
fetishes 65
Fiji 24
fire 24, 26
Flower Remedies 87
flowers 86–7
frankincense 90
future: foretelling 145–6

Gabon 76
gender disguise 105
Ghana 123, 154, 163
Ghost Dance 115
girls: puberty ritual 120
Great Spirit 40–1
Greeks 66, 80, 82
Greenland 21, 22, 105, 111
guardians 34–5
Guatemala 55, 148
guides, spirit 34
Gundestrup cauldron 66, 67

Hatshepsut 90
Hausa 127
Hawaii 120, 137, 153
healing:
    plants 85, 88–9
    songs for 108, 109
    through dancing 115

herbs 88–9
hermaphrodites 128
Hindus 27
Hmong 37, 122, 126, 136, 145
Hong Kong 122
Hopi 28, 122–3, 141, 144
    symbols 139
Huichol 64, 84, 85, 104, 141, 144,
    152, 157
    animals and 48
    pilgrimage 14
    plant use 79
    sacred sites 18
    shapeshifting 68
Hungary 126
hunting 44–7

Iban 129, 144
Igbo 60, 146, 148
illness:
    diagnosis 156–7
    extracting 158–9
    route to shamanism 122
Inca 18, 76, 89
incense 90–3
India 136
Indonesia 112
Inga 78
initiation 60, 122–3
Inua 66
Inuit 24, 34, 46, 65, 66, 111, 114,
    127, 132, 136
    fishing 44–5
    mask 137
Iroquois 71, 80, 117
Isis 24

jaguar 50, 51, 53
Janai Purnima: pilgrims 15, 15
Japan 13, 26, 27, 32, 99, 116, 126,
    132, 154
Java 89, 137
jimsonweed 79, 85

Kabouti, Fred 138
Kaikha 99

Kailash 20
Kalahari Desert 41
Kanaimà 134
Kangjiashimenzi 128
Karelia 40
Kauyumári 152
Kazakh 111, 156
Khakass 116, 135
knife: ritual 132
Kogi 68, 123, 162, 163
Kokopelli 111
Korea 33, 117, 121, 126, 129, 138
Krahó 78
Kuna 109
!Kung 46, 112, 134, 158, 160
Kwakwaka'wakw 55
Kyrgyzstan 54

La Rumorosa 23
Ladakhi 145
Lakota 22, 23, 27, 32, 96–7, 104,
    115, 120, 129
Lao Tzu 10
Laos 37, 104, 122, 136, 145
Lapland 145
Lascaux caves 22
Lebcou 158
ley lines 14
lightning 22
Linnaeus, Carl 87

Madagascar 80
Mahu 129
Malaysia 97
Mali 111
Mama Wata 26
Manchu 24, 111, 116
Manchuria 137
mandalas 138
Maori 10
    symbols 140
Mapuche 49, 88, 129, 147, 162
marginality 127
masks 69, 70–1, 70, 80, 80, 137
Master of the Animals 66–7, 67
May Day 117

Maya 12, 15, 28, 52–3, 81, 100,
    104, 146, 148
Mazateco 56
Mecca 18
medicine wheels 29
Meitei 97
metal 27
Mevlevi 112
Mexico 23, 36, 55, 93, 109, 141,
    144, 148, 157
    Day of the Dead 116–17,
    118–19
midsummer 116
mineral 27
mirrors 146
mistletoe 84
Mistress of the Animals 66–7
Mohave 128
Mongolia 28, 29, 99, 104, 136,
    137, 163
Monument Valley, Utah 12
morals 135
mountains 26, 32
mummies 152, 152
mummification 92–3
Murut 23, 137
music 110–11
Muslims 138, 156
myrrh 90
mythical creatures 62–3

Nagano: waterfalls 25
Nähñu 36, 37, 77, 89, 93, 157
Naskapi 46
nature 21–3
Navajo 10, 11, 22–3, 29, 36, 65,
    138
Nazca: drum 111
Ndembu 37, 161
Nepal 33, 36, 37, 89, 107, 116, 127
    pilgrimages 15, 15
New Year 117
Newgrange 141
Ngungi 126
Nguni 65
Niger 33, 127, 146

Nigeria 110, 127, 148
Nong 123

objects, power 142–4
Odin 127, 128
offering bowl 104
offerings: making 102–4
Ojibwa 24, 96, 115, 148
Okinawa 99
Olmec 58
    sculpture 58
Orokaiva 120, 121
Oroqen 80, 117
otherworld:
    costume 107
    dismemberment in 130–3
    landscapes 32–3
    levels 32–3
    portals to 81
    spirits and guardians in
    34–5
    travel to 30–3, 81
    voyage through 130–1

Pachamama 102
Pacific Islands 13
Paiute 115
Panama 109
Papua New Guinea 70, 120, 147,
    148, 152, 160
Pazyryk tribe 62
Peru 89, 108, 120–1, 126, 135,
    142, 156, 158, 163
pets: as power animals 61
peyote cactus 74–5, 77, 79, 84
pilgrimage 13–15
    directions 28, 29
    to experience elements 26
    preparation for 13–14
    route 13–14
Pima 109
place: spirits of 35
plants:
    meeting 79
    sacred 74–7
    spirits of 78–9

Pliny the Elder 84
Plutarch 90
Pomo 153
possession 154–5
Potnia Theron 66
power:
    channelling 20
    from directions 29
power animals 56–8, 79
    finding 58
    masks of 70–1
    pets as 61
    shapeshifting into 68–71
power objects 142–4, 143, 144
prayer flags 19
prayer service 112–13
protection: gaining 136–7
puberty: rituals 120
Puha 149

Q'ero 102
qi energy: flow of 10
Qiang 65

Rai 37
Rajasthan 154
Rarámuri 93, 162
Rasmussen, Knud 46
rites of passage 120–1
rituals 96–123
    for bedtime 101
    costume for 105–7
    creating 97, 98, 99, 117
    for everyday life 99–101
    healing 93
    offerings 102–4
    plants used 76–7
    sample 98
    on waking 99
rivers: north-flowing 32
rock art see cave and rock art
rogi 55
roundhouses 10

sacred objects 36
sacred sites 13, 18–20
    boundaries 19–20
    elements at 24–7
    focusing techniques 21–2

taking objects from 36
    visiting 18–20
sacred symbols 138–41, 139, 140
sacrifice 59–61, 104
Sakha 129
salmon: swimming 116
Samhain 117
Sámi 40, 44–6, 48, 77, 78, 81,
    108, 145
San Pedro cactus 77
Sánchez, José Bénitez 74
Santería 10–12, 110, 111, 114, 154
Santiago de Compostela 14
scent: in ceremony 92–3
Scythians 48–9
Seahenge 71
seasonal celebrations 116–17
seasons: directions and 29
Semai 35, 86, 122
Senegal 158
sexuality 128–9
shapeshifting 67, 68–71
Shasta 156
Shipbo 142
Shipibo-Conibo 108, 157
Shor 110, 111
Shoshone: Sun Dance 117
shrines: creating 36–7
Shuar 32, 34, 76, 120–1, 134,
    156, 158, 163
Sibe 137
Siberia 33, 34, 47, 53, 70, 81, 107,
    110, 116, 129
    shamanic flags 57
    shepherd 61
Sibundoy valley 78
Sioux 96–7, 104, 115, 120
Skolt Sámi 40
smudging 93
snuff 76
solstices 28
songlines 13, 16
songs 108–9
Sora people 12
souls:
    animal/human exchange 47
    retrieval 160–1
spatulamancy 145
spirit helpers: animals 50–3

spirits 34–5
    animal 41
    calling to shamanism 122
    communication with 96–7
    extraction 158–9
    plant 78–9
    possession by 154–5
    protection from 136–7
    songs 108–9
    submission to 130–3
    tree 80
spring: rituals 117
stone rubbing 21
Stonehenge 28, 116
Sudan 145
suffering 122–3, 126
sun 23, 26, 28
Sun Dance 117
sweat lodge ceremony 27
symbols 138–41, 139, 140

taboo 136, 156
Tacitus 145
Taíno 76
Taiwan 145
Tajikistan 158
Taleutians 107
talismans 138
Taman 122, 132, 134, 148, 164
Tamang 36
Tantric Buddhism 132
tarantism 115
Teleutians 33
Thailand 37, 102, 104, 122, 136,
    145, 154, 157
theatre 97
Tibet 88, 107, 138, 143, 158, 161
    prayer flags 19
    sacred sites 18–19, 20
time 12
Tlingit: power object 143
Tmimshian 146
Toba 122, 135, 149, 156
tobacco 79, 84
totems 140
    animal 54–5
trance 6, 30–3, 30–1, 110
    inducing 74
    music and 112–14

transgender 128
trees 80–2
tricksters: animal spirits 53
Tsugaru 64, 65, 116
Tuareg 115
Tudlik: painting 34, 35
Tukano 68
Tupí 50
Tuva 111
Tuvan people 7, 18, 35, 62, 65

Uluru 36, 37
Ute 147
Uyghur 137, 158
Uzbek 158

Varanesi 20
Venus 20
visions: quest for 21, 23
Voudou 88, 154, 155

Waalo kingdom 49
waking: rituals 99
walkabout 13
water 24, 26
web of life 10–12, 14–15, 20
Wicca 117
Wirikuta 14, 84, 85
Witsen, Nicolaas 6
wood 27
World Tree 81

Xhosa 65, 132

Yaka 122, 123
Yakut 107, 110
Yaminahua 108
Yggdrasil 81
Yokut tribe 55
Yoruba 110
Yuman 108, 144, 148
Yurok 128–9

Zafimaniry 80
Zambia 37
Zarma 154
Zulu 53, 54, 65, 81, 126, 145–6,
    147, 148
Zuni 65, 77

AUTHOR ACKNOWLEDGMENTS

It is always a pleasure acknowledging people who contribute to my writing but, for this book more than others, it is to the traditional shamans and spiritual practitioners who have kept the tradition alive for me to practise and write about in the 21st century, that I owe my greatest debt. As I was completing the text, word reached me of 14 shamans in South America who have been murdered for their beliefs. Their deaths add to a depressing total across the ages and remind us, if any reminder is needed, that shamanism only exists today because of the devotion and dedication of people who, quite literally, give their lives to preserve it.

With the dramatic loss of shamanic tradition during the last century, much wisdom is now stored in ethnographic and anthropological reports. For access to these, I am grateful to the librarians of the Sackler and Bodleian Libraries in Oxford. The librarians of the Radcliffe Science Library, also in Oxford, have helped immensely with references on the human mind and trance states. Libraries are treasure houses of wisdom, and I am truly grateful for the time I can spend in them.

This book started as a discussion with Sandra Rigby of Watkins, and her encouragement and enthusiasm for the book have been awesome ever since. It was a pleasure to work with Fiona Robertson and Suzanne Tuhrim on the layout and with Jane McIntosh on the detailed edit and the book has improved greatly as a result. My agent Susan Mears has been brilliant, as always.

Writing can be lonely at times and I am grateful for all my colleagues and friends on Twitter and on my Facebook page who keep me going. They provide the "water-cooler" moments that get me through the day. In particular, Ishtar Dingir, Melissa Heavener, Holly Hughes, Neil Ingram, Maggie Macnab, Zena Romano, Jason Smalley, Peter Stockinger, Luitha Tamaya, Ticia Verveer, Alex Webley, Julie Wheeler, and Nancy Wiser

have especially supported my research and work. Nick Wood runs the best shamanic magazine going – *Sacred Hoop* – and is a valued help.

I am particularly grateful to Kirsti Bambridge, Deirdre Gough, David Mason, Niillas Somby, Christina Ward-Large, Luba Zhalsanov, and Marina Zhigzhitova who all provided information for my work.

Emily Jones is always there at just the right time and has been a massive support and influence throughout the writing of this book.

My students and, increasingly, ex-students as they complete their training, from the Order of Bards, Ovates and Druids are fabulous and provide so much inspiration that I often wonder who is teaching whom. Vicki Minahan was always one of the best and she gently influences my work with her love of shamanism and deerhounds.

It might be appropriate at this point to acknowledge Mabon and Cafall, my deerhounds and constant companions as I write. Megan, the cat I share my life with, waits for me to finish with the impatience that 22 years of life has earned her.

My wife Vanessa has been the centre of my world for all my adult life; I could not conceive of attempting anything without her love to sustain me.

My own brush with traditional shamans occurred in Siberia and Lapland where Debbie Wander was my travelling companion, confidante, anthropological assistant, and – as she would doubtless concur – maid and general dogsbody. It is a wonder we are still such close friends but thankfully we are. This book is dedicated to her in memory of the times we spent laughing, crying, and cowering in a yurt on the side of a sacred mountain while a group of Russian soldiers fought a running battle outside. Спасибо!

PICTURE CREDITS

176

Page 1 Musée du quai Branl, Patrick Gries/Scala; 2 John Mitchell/Alamy; 7 Ilya Naymushin/Corbis; 8–9 Cyril Russo/J H Editorial/Getty Images; 10 SSPL/Getty Images; 12 Luis Castaneda/Tips/Axiom; 15 Sunil Sharma/Demotix/Corbis; 16–17 Günter Lenz/FotoLibra; 19 Ian Cumming/Axiom; 21 BAL/Getty Images; 22 Chris Howes/Wild Places Photography/Alamy; 25 Muneo Abe/Getty Images; 26–7 Darrell Gulin/Corbis; 30–31 © Don Pablo Amaringo/North Atlantic Books; 35 Public Trustee for Nunavut, Estate of Tudlik/National Gallery of Canada, Ottawa, Photo © NGC; 37 Colin Mattieu/Hemis/Axiom; 38–9 Joel Sartore Photography; 42–3 Daniel J Cox/Stone/Getty; 44–5 Victor Ekootak Estate, Canadian Arctic Producers Library and Holman Eskimo Co-op Ltd/Collection of the Winnipeg Art Gallery, Gift of Indian & Northern Affairs, Canada, Accession #: G-89-630, Ernest Mayer/Winnipeg Art Gallery; 46 Public Trustee for Nunavut, Estate of David Ikuutaq/Collection of the Winnipeg Art Gallery, Gift of Dr. Harry Winrob, Accession #: 2006-594.1 to 5/Ernest Mayer/Winnipeg Art Gallery; 49 Paul Souders/Corbis; 51 Panoramic Images/Getty Images; 52 © Kenojuak Ashevak Estate/reproduced with the permissions of Dorset Fine Arts/ Collection of the Winnipeg Art Gallery.Gift of Indian & Northern Affairs, Canada, Accession #: G-89-630/Ernest Mayer, Winnipeg Art Gallery, Canada; 55 Ron Watts/Corbis; 57 Bruno Morandi/The Image Bank/Getty Images; 58 WFA/ Dallas Museum of Art, USA; 60–61 Philip Lee Harvey /Axiom; 63 © Trustees of the British Museum; 67 WFA/National Museum, Copenhagen; 69 John Frumm/Hemis/Axiom; 70 WFA/Schindler Collection, New York ; 72–3 Pete Oxford/Minden Pictures/Getty Images; 74–5 © Courtesy of the Estate of Benitez Sanchez/Courtesy of the Penn Museum, Image: 148701 97-15-1; 78 Dozier Marc/Hemis. Fr/Alamy; 80 Armand J. Labbe/Bowers Museum, USA/Corbis; 82–3 Jeremy Woodhouse/Image Bank/Getty Images; 85 Art Gallery and Museum, Kelvingrove, Glasgow, Scotland/© Culture and Sport Glasgow (Museums)/BAL; 91 Hugh Sitton/Photographer's Choice/Corbis; 94–5 Milwaukee Art Museum, Gift of Richard and Erna Flagg M1991.127/Efraim Lev-er; 96 Moon Yin Lam/Alamy; 100 John Warden/Photolibrary/Getty Images; 103 Luis Castaneda/Tips/Axiom; 104 Courtesy of the Penn Museum, Image: 152509 38-23-122; 106 Thomas L. Kelly/Axiom; 111 AA/Museo Larco Herrera , Lima; 112–13 Estate of Everald Brown/Wayne and Myrene Cox Collection; 117 The Stapleton Collection/BAL; 118–19 Sergio Ballivian/Axiom, 122 WFA/Formerly Philip Goldman Collection, London; 124–5 © Estate of Ginger Tjakamarra/DACS London, 2012/BAL; 127 WFA/Statens Historiska Museum, Stockholm; 130–31 © Estate of Roy de Forest/DACS, London/VAGA, New York, 2012/BAL; 132 WFA/Private collection, London; 137 WFA/Eugene Chestow Trust; 139 Tom Bean/Corbis; 140 Andrea Pistolesi/Tips/Axiom; 143 WFA/Private Collection; 144 WFA/British Museum, London; 146 Musée du quai Branly, Patrick Gries/Scala, Florence; 147 Ross Land/Getty Images; 150–51 Arthur Morris/Corbis; 152 Chris Rainier/Corbis; 155 Mireille Vautier; 160 Seattle Art Museum, USA/Corbis